Embellishments

CONSTRUCTING VICTORIAN DETAIL

ASTRIDA SCHAEFFER

2013
SchaefferArts Costume Exhibition & Care
North Berwick, Maine

Printed in Canada

ISBN13: 978-1-938394-04-1
Library of Congress Control Number: 2013937871

Published and designed by:
Great Life Press
www.greatlifepress.com

Additional copies available from:
SchaefferArts Costume Exhibition & Care
67 Meehan Lane
North Berwick, Maine 03906

www.schaefferarts.com

Photo Credits: Photography of garments in the Irma Bowen Textile Collection by permission of the University Museum, University of New Hampshire.

Cover: Walking dress, c. 1880, silk, satin and taffeta, Irma Bowen Textile Collection, University Museum, Accession No. 57. Photography courtesy Brian Smestad.

To Dale Valena, for setting me on this road.

Contents

Plates

Acknowledgments

Having an idea is one thing—watching a team of energetic, creative people respond to it enthusiastically, believe in it despite the odds, and work so hard to make it happen is humbling. This project began with a request to teach Victorian handwork techniques, grew into a full-blown exhibition, and blossomed into this book. I could not have done it alone.

As an independent scholar it is a joy to be welcomed to work on a collection, and Dale Valena has been letting me loose on the treasures in the University Museum at the University of New Hampshire for over a decade. Thank you, Dale, for giving my love of historic clothing a direction and for believing that hosting a costume exhibition is a great idea.

Thank you to Janith Bergeron for encouraging me to pull these ideas about Victorian embellishment together and teach them to fellow textile enthusiasts of all ages. What began as teaching notes kept going.

Special thanks to the team at Silk Damask Consulting—without their hard work, dedication and talents this book would not have been possible. Kimberly Alexander's unstoppable drive and passion for the subject and Jeffrey Hopper's deep well of knowledge and attention to detail so beautifully helped crystallize the concept. Thanks also to Bridget Swift, whose research assistance was invaluable. Questions need answers!

For that fresh look when I'd been staring at things for too long—thank you to Tara Vose Raiselis, director of the Saco Museum, for reading the manuscript and helping clarify it for readers who weren't quite so buried in the subject matter.

For the lovely photography filling these pages I would like to thank Lisa Nugent and Brian Smestad, both of whom brought a true artist's eye to the material. I am grateful also to the UNH Center for the Humanities for their support of the book's photography.

I would like to especially thank Grace Peirce of Great Life Press for stepping in and bringing her talent and wonderful eye to bear on this project, taking the work of so many and crafting it into the beautiful form you hold in your hands.

For graciously sharing her proofreader's eagle eye, many thanks to Linda Conti, mentor and friend.

Encouragement and support come in many forms, and for providing them so generously and enthusiastically I thank my parents, Yvonne Borowska and Witold Mechlinski. It seems to be working!

And, as always, to my husband, Stephen, and daughter Helena, thank you for putting up with me when the midnight oil was burning yet again. In so many ways, thank you.

Foreword

The Milne Special Collections and University Museum of the University of New Hampshire are rich with treasures quirky and sublime, and few more so than the Irma Bowen Collection. Now, thanks to Astrida Schaeffer's *Embellishments: Constructing Victorian Detail*, we are able to showcase this premier collection of Victorian fashion. The volume is itself rich with details quirky and sublime: the careful specificity of box pleats and knife pleats; the focus on ruching at the hem of a garment; the satisfying vocabulary of braiding, piping, ruffles, scallops, cord and collar, appliqué and passementerie. With this stunning volume, the first to showcase our Collections, and the combined talents of faculty and staff at the University Museum, Dimond Library, the Department of History, and Photographic Services, the University is thrilled to offer scholars, students, devotees of fabric culture and fashion, and readers from all walks of life a densely layered look at the wearable art of the Victorians.

April 2013, Durham, New Hampshire

Lisa MacFarlane, PhD
Senior Vice Provost for Academic Affairs
Professor of English and American Studies
University of New Hampshire

Introduction

The history of the Victorian Age will never be written:
we know too much about it.

—Lytton Strachey

Lytton Strachey (1880–1932), a founding member of the Bloomsbury group of writers and intellectuals, and author of *Eminent Victorians* (1918) and *Queen Victoria* (1921), was certainly in a position to make this claim. Strachey's enigmatic conclusion was not off the mark, and the Victorian influence that came to define the late nineteenth century remains an epoch that confounds historians and scholars. For the modern audience, the term "Victorian" is one that implies much and reveals little simultaneously, often conjuring up an image of "being surrounded by exquisite clutter," as Freddie Mercury of *Queen* memorably described in 1977.

The nineteenth century certainly was a period of cultural clutter, as the three sisters of modern life—industrialization, immigration, and urbanization—excited and disturbed the rhythms of society and family. Fashion frequently sought to organize this clutter, both triggering and mirroring the "tyranny of change," as one historian has described this maelstrom of unsettling forces. Singer's sewing machines enabled women to experiment with trends inside the home. *The Delineator* and other design journals excited their hopes and guided their hands by introducing Chicago and Omaha to current patterns from Paris and London. *Godey's Lady's Book* and other magazines that catered expressly to women and inspired them to develop themselves as domestic paragons. Catalogues like those of Sears, Roebuck allowed them to make purchases from virtually anywhere in the United States.

It is no small irony, then, that the figure whose name represents this period of exquisite clutter presented herself as an adamantine force of tradition and decorum. Queen Victoria would be Britain's longest ruling monarch, ascending the throne in 1837 and holding court until 1901. But, it was marriage in 1840 to Prince Albert of Saxe-Coburg and Gotha that marked a dramatic shift in the idea of fashion. Not unlike the royal weddings of today, her dress was watched carefully—on both sides of the Atlantic. Designed by William Dyce (who was head of what became known as the Royal College of Art) and stitched by Mary Bettans (one of Queen Victoria's skilled dressmakers) the gown was enriched with English Honiton lace and, notably, white, inspiring a tradition in wedding fashion that persists to this day. *Godey's* editor Sarah Hale saw an opportunity and filled the magazine with Lydia H. Sigourney's accounts of court life in London that inspired American women to imitate a royalty that their politics denied them.

The historic garments captured here, many published for the first time, date from the late Victorian period, roughly 1875 until 1909. As such, they reveal complications of nationalism and homage to European trends in fashion that Americans found displayed in the great international expositions of their day. The dresses created in the post-Civil War period and on the eve of the American Centennial Exposition in Philadelphia are not as distant from the direct influence of Queen Victoria's court and Parisian haute couture as one might expect. By the first decade of the twentieth century, however, the American woman was frequently dictating style to meet her own special needs. In a fast-paced culture of technology—where sewing machines for the home were available and clothing patterns were disseminated widely—new freedom and creativity surfaced.

Therefore, it is not surprising to see the influence of the Colonial Revival (Plate 7, p. 64) in a gown inspired by the American Centennial Exhibition, the structured high style elegance of the mid 1880s in a dress worn by Miss Nims (Plate 6, p. 56) or Celestia's Homemade Dress (Plate 1, p. 4) all debuting within a year or two of one another.

The clothing worn by women of the period is of especial interest and continues to fascinate—beyond the curiosity of the corsetry and bustles. To the contemporary viewer, the need for full ensembles for different functions, frequently requiring several entire changes throughout the day, combined with the constant changing of styles, colors and accessories for different seasons, may be, on the surface, confusing. The seemingly endless hours of effort and expense spent creating the perfect, most exquisitely tailored garments, literally dripping with yard upon yard of braid, draping, piping and pleating can appear excessive, or to return to Freddie Mercury, "cluttered." And yet to the Victorian eye, our fashion selections today would seem remarkably unfinished and plain. Indeed, for all the influence we now ascribe to Queen Victoria's wedding gown, many of her contemporaries considered it too conservative and old fashioned, not befitting of royalty.

Although collected as a pedagogical tool for those learning sewing techniques, Irma Bowen also created a lasting pean to the international fashion scene and the burgeoning role of American women in that milieu, particularly American modifications of the last quarter of the nineteenth century to the first decades of the twentieth. The collection featured in this book falls almost entirely between two major world fairs: the American 1876 Centennial Exhibition and the 1900 Exposition Universelle (widely known for giving voice to the Art Nouveau style). Many of the gowns reflect the progressive fashions associated with these events. The Expositions themselves also were opportunities to share news back home. Attendance at the 1889 Paris Exposition Universelle was not unlike an international "who's who," see and be seen. For example, Princess Alexandra (Plate 3, p. 18) attended and would have carried her distinctive and eagerly sought style with her to a thirsty and appreciative international, star-studded audience.

The sound associated with the sweep of bustled taffeta, the crinkle of crepe, or the swish of a floor length train would not be lost on a drawing room audience. Indeed, some garments were intended to be viewed as much from the back as from the front with fully gathered bustles, drapes and bows, trim, braid and tassels which would attract attention to the gait of the wearer, with the almost hypnotizing tempo of a short train. And yet, being surrounded by yards of fabric and accessories such as fans and parasols kept others at a distance. In the 1870s, some commentators noted that the tailoring over waist and hips so accentuated the female form that it was nothing short of scandalous. It is important to consider that the manner in which the garments were worn was as much a part of how they were to be seen and how they displayed the wearer. As Charles Frederick Worth (1825–1895), revered as the leader of the era's most respected and sought after haute couture designs, confided to *Harper's Bazar* 15 December 1877: "A dress should never overpower its wearer. It should merely be an appropriate frame for a charming picture.... It isn't every woman who knows how to wear a dress."

Closing the nineteenth century, L'Heure Bleue: A Gown of Midnight Blue Velvet (Plate 10, p. 96) embodies a number of design trends: the astonishing passementerie, voided velvet and cording brings to mind motifs of American architects Louis Sullivan and Frank Lloyd Wright as well as the vibrant use of light and technology of the 1889 Paris Universelle with its iconic Eiffel Tower.

Launching the twentieth century, the 1893 World's Columbian Exposition showcased countless changes in American life and lifestyle from the debut of Cracker Jack® and shredded wheat, to the wonders of electric lighting and complex water systems. Americans attended the World's Columbian Exposition in Chicago in droves with over 20 million visitors. What they saw fascinated them—an organized city with electric light cables buried beneath the ground, coordinated water and transportation systems. This grand city, the White City, would lead to the explosion of the City Beautiful Movement. Women comprised a major portion of the audience, many visiting Boston architect and MIT graduate Sophia Hayden's Women's Building, with examples of women's success highlighted throughout.

Embellishments is a fashion time travelers' armchair tour. With the absence of narration from those who wore or owned the clothing shown throughout this book, consider the historic garments themselves as your guide. Follow respected costume historian and author Astrida Schaeffer through the steps of creating the embellishments that adorn each gown; savor the stunning photography of Brian Smestad and Lisa Nugent as the nineteenth century unfolds, draws to a close, and the twentieth opens with promise.

Kimberly Alexander, PhD
History Department, Visiting Faculty
University of New Hampshire, Durham

Godey's Lady's Book, *December 1864*

1

The Victorian Aesthetic Mindset

*At present trimmings are used with a profusion that
is little short of extravagant... Frequently a costume is
enriched with two or more kinds of garniture, and if the
mode of disposal is tasteful, the variety of ornamentation
gives no hint of exaggeration... [A] bodice may be adorned
with fur, lace, and either ribbon or jet, all of which
trimmings are thoroughly congenial.*

—*The Delineator*, December 1894

Rich colors, lavish textures, layers of lush fabrics and delicate detail—beautiful, ornate women's clothes are the visual icons of the nineteenth century, so much so that "embellishment" is almost a definition for "Victorian style." To embellish something, to transform it with decoration and then add more, is at the core of the era's understanding of beauty, a celebration of the thing itself. There was plenty to embellish; for the industrialized world, the nineteenth century saw an explosion of goods available to more people in more places than ever before. It is the name of Britain's Queen Victoria, who ruled an expanding empire from 1837–1901, which has come to describe this era of elaborate ornamentation on everything from clothing to furnishings to architecture. The aesthetic grew out of colonial contact with cultures from around the world as well as the exciting technologies, discoveries, and opportunities bursting out of the Industrial Revolution. New materials, new colors, new production methods! With all these abundant options available, why use one type of trim when you could use five?

In 2012, the exhibition *Embellishments: Constructing Victorian Detail* opened at the University of New Hampshire (UNH). This publication showcases the beautifully detailed garments gathered for the installation and provides a guide to further exploration of design and techniques.

The Irma Bowen Textile Collection at UNH was originally assembled in the early twentieth century as a teaching tool for dressmakers. Irma Bowen acquired most of the pieces as instructional examples for her sewing classes in the home economics department, and the collection continued to grow for some time after her retirement in the 1930s before becoming part of the University Museum in 1947. While few, if any, identifying records accompanied them, donations came predominantly from surrounding communities. This book renews the collection's original educational purpose, while providing access to previously unpublished garments as inspiration for contemporary textile arts enthusiasts. First you will "learn to see" how over-the-top examples of extravagant fashion are in fact a series of simple pieces combined for a fabulous effect. Then you can learn how to make those pieces yourself, with diagrams and detailed photographs of construction elements giving you an intimate close-up look.

By Victorian standards, today's clothing is relatively plain and unadorned. Though the sheer volume of ornamentation can seem endless and more than a bit daunting, Victorian couture holds a wealth of design ideas that can be easily applied to personalize your look and enhance your contemporary style. Examined closely, the aesthetic really breaks down into the five main elements discussed in this chapter:

Self Trim
Color Contrast
Texture Contrast
Asymmetry
Layering Elements

These five key design elements underlie all the manipulated fabric trims that follow later in the book. There are literally hundreds of ways these basic techniques were used in the nineteenth century, more than any one costume collection can illustrate. The goal is to inspire you, to provide a springboard for your own ideas and explorations. Take what you learn here, look at clothing in other publications and exhibitions with new eyes, and see what other variations on these embellishments you can find. Whether simply for the joy of understanding them better or to apply the techniques to your own work, learning to think like a Victorian designer is the first step to unpacking the process behind these clothes and their richly vibrant aesthetic.

Self Trim

One of the most common techniques found in Victorian embellishment design is to use the same fabric as that of the dress as trim, or self trim. Strips of ruching, knife pleats, or box pleats are created and applied to the garment, individually or in combination (fig. 1). Box pleats are occasionally folded into three or more layers deep and then further manipulated into fanciful shapes.

Having more than one fabric with which to make trimmings increases the possible visual effect, but the embellishments are still made from material already on hand for the main construction of the garment. One of the more elaborate dresses in this book, the brown and taupe gown in figure 2, has no decoration or trim at all except for the pleats, edge bindings, ruchings, and bands made of its own two silks.

In some cases the design of the material itself offers clear embellishment opportunities (fig. 3, Plate 10). The fabric of this gown is already spectacular, a deep midnight blue velvet pile woven on a red ground that causes the fabric to shimmer with exposed color when it moves. Broad bands where the velvet pile has been omitted in the weaving process expose intricate patterns of red ground. This is the ultimate self trim example, as the strong vertical stripes are carefully manipulated with darts to shape the bodice so that it looks as if the curving shape was woven. The dress speaks of luxury from its fabric all the way through to its tailoring.

FIG. 1. *Detail of box pleat and knife pleat combination trim, see Plate 3 (p. 18).*

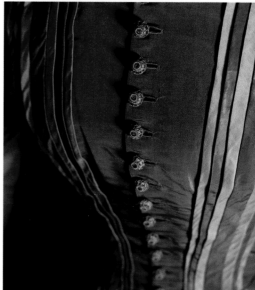

FIG. 2. *Gown made of two fabrics, using both to make self trim, see Plate 6 (p. 56).*

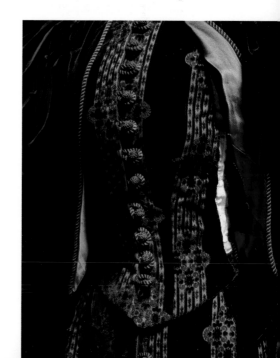

FIG. 3. *Close up of the dart shaping the bodice, and of the thrifty use of expensive materials on the bodice front and "jacket" lining. See Plate 10 (p. 96).*

Plate 1
The Reign of the Sewing Machine Begins: Celestia's Homemade Dress
Early 1870s
Silk faille with silk satin and fringe

Comprised of bodice, underskirt, overskirt, and separate collar with detailed fringe, this gown reflects home sewing and the widespread availability of fashion plates and patterns during the waning decades of the nineteenth century. For all its high style attributes, a number of characteristics point to it being homemade. Buttonholes are too small, the tailoring is a little clumsy, and the overall finishing of the dress does not compare to professionally-made garments of the time, making it a fascinating object of study.

Celestia Freeman, a Somersworth, New Hampshire, mill overseer's wife, likely made this dress, the styling of which, despite its amateur seamstress errors, speaks to a certain status. She would have had access to a sewing machine to make it as these were available for home use by the end of the 1850s, and manufacturers had introduced lease-to-purchase plans that made machines readily accessible and certainly within the means of the middle-class Freeman family. In addition to the sewing machine itself, the wide scale availability of patterns transformed the opportunities for home sewing by the 1870s. As early as 1867, Ebenezer Butterick was distributing patterns through magazines, introducing the popular *Delineator* in 1873. Fashion magazines such as Butterick's as well as *Harper's Bazar* and *Godey's Lady's Book* would also have been readily available to her, so Celestia's inspirations for this dress could have been legion (see Appendix, Celestia's Inspiration, p. 105).

The dress displays a solid grounding in the Victorian design mindset. The bodice, underskirt, and overskirt are made of a pale grey ribbed silk (faille), as are the ruffles, bands, and pleats decorating it. The lovely matching separate collar is trimmed with knife pleats of the same fabric. The details of the dress are then highlighted with a contrasting texture and color in the form of a steely blue silk satin used as piping and edging, and finished off with a silk fringe on the collar and cuffs. The cuffs show an extra detail often found in later Victorian trims: a box pleat accent with origami-like folded-down edges forming diamonds, an innovation influenced by the Victorian fascination with Japan. Given the wear it shows, this must have been Celestia's favorite dress.

Bowen Collection, University Museum,
Accession No. 114, Gift of B. Freeman
See also Figs. 4, 11, 51, 77, 79, 145

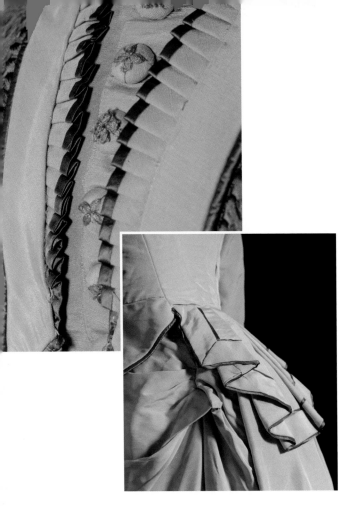

FIG. 4A-B, *details of Plate 1 (p. 4). Above: collar made of self-trim knife pleats edged with a contrasting color. Inset: trimmed skirting on the back of the bodice.*

FIG. 5. *Back of gown showing how the intricate build up of two colors creates the impression of a much more elaborate fabric. See Plate 6 (p. 56).*

Color Contrast

Another popular Victorian technique is to contrast one color with another. The contrast can be strong, as in figure 4 where the use of a steel blue color "pops" an element that might otherwise visually disappear. For example the collar's knife pleats are made of the same pale fabric as the dress but edged with blue to finish them. The effect is to outline the gown and draw attention to key places where the seamstress manipulated her fabric, turning the garment's rather drab color into a canvas of interesting shapes (especially fig. 77, p. 52).

Not all color contrasts need to be so extreme, and can be achieved with colors in the same tone family. In figure 5, the primary underlying design motif is the alternation of color. This exceptionally lovely brown and taupe gown is simply decorated with the two fabrics used to construct the bodice and skirts, both plain woven silks. There is no additional trim on the dress other than that created out of the material itself. A lush, rich effect occurs because each color sets off the other.

Outlining elements form combinations with each other in alternating tones, which emphasize the tiny waist and flowing lines of the skirt. Narrow strips of one color of fabric are used to trim portions of the other. Broad strips are pleated to finish the edges of the various levels of the skirts. Each piece of applied fabric is set at a different angle to the ground fabric, so light itself becomes part of the gown's design in a most intriguing way—as it plays across the complex sheen of alternating bias and straight grain silks. When worn and in motion, this aspect of the gown would have been even more eye catching, surely as the designer intended.

6

Texture Contrast

Texture is as important as color and the combinations can be quite subtle, as in figure 6. This day gown uses two fabrics in very similar colors, one incorporating a plain matte taffeta finish and the other a smooth satin finish. The combined effect is quite luxurious, with the alternating textures constructed in complex layers across the gown's skirts emphasizing asymmetry. As with Plate 6 (p. 56), the opulence comes solely from two unadorned fabrics used together.

Figure 7 shows three different textures working together to beautiful effect. Chandler & Co. of Boston produced this elegant blue wool suit with a blue velvet collar and woven blue cord. Applied to the collar, buttons, and panels of the coat and skirt, the cording's complex braided surface and slight sheen bring visual interest to the suit. The tailoring is lovely, but it is the combination of these three different textures that creates a vibrant ensemble.

Figure 8 shows a very common yet striking use of texture contrast: a decorative bow made of the dress's silk fabric paired with velvet. The motif of a two-texture bow shows up repeatedly in Victorian design, sometimes even in different combinations on the same garment.

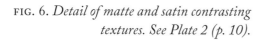

FIG. 6. *Detail of matte and satin contrasting textures. See Plate 2 (p. 10).*

FIG. 7. *Collar and cord made with a contrasting texture to the suit. See Plate 8 (p. 72).*

FIG. 8. *Detail of skirt bow from the 1870s, watered silk and velvet, owned by Sawyer-Ffrost, Accession No. 227.*

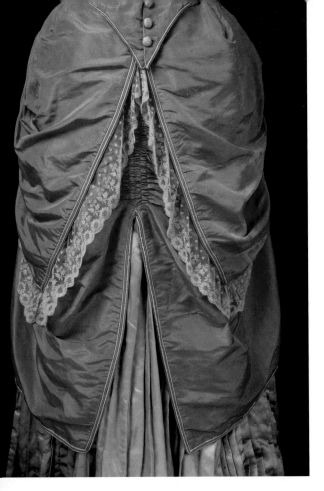

FIG. 9. *Piping, lace, ruching, pleats, contrasting colors and textures—this dress has a little bit of everything. See Plate 7 (p. 64).*

Layering Elements

One embellishment was rarely enough for the Victorians and even the simplest dresses often incorporated multiple elements. The golden silk taffeta gown in figure 9 is edged with four alternating rows of piping made of a contrasting pale blue satin and of the dress fabric itself. Soft ruffles of lace fall from the hem of the overskirt, neckline, and sleeves. Pale blue pleated silk satin fills in the front of the gown's skirt, with matching blue silk-covered buttons closing the bodice. Pleats of the primary dress fabric finish the hem of the train. Even the overskirt itself is designed in layers for a triple skirt effect.

This layering can also be achieved with subtle texture. Figure 10 shows a Parisian wool gown made by the design house of Maison Rouff at the turn of the century, and it is a confit of multiple kinds of lace, netting overlays, cord work, silk roses and silk pleated frond ribbon work. The fine wool fabric of the gown frames the very different textures of each of these decorative elements, all in a monochromatic creamy ivory that nonetheless achieves a lush visual whole.

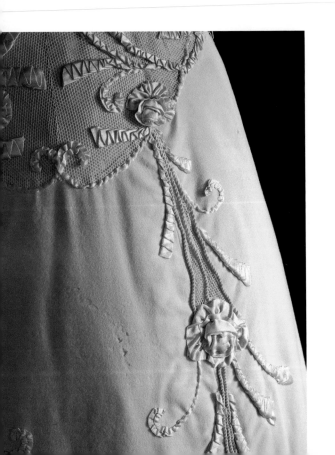

FIG. 10. *Waist detail of gown, showing a variety of materials and techniques. See Plate 5.*

The gown in figure 11 is of particular interest as it is homemade. Its workmanship is very different from high end, professionally produced clothing of the time (see Plate 2, p. 10 for comparison), however it shows how a woman of limited means could still apply the design aesthetic of her day to look her best. The layering of elements is central to the statement this dress makes about the respectable status of the wearer. With all its many frills and treatments, this is no common laborer's gown! This garment has self-trim bands on the cuffs, folded-back effects on the overskirt, ruffles and pleats on the main skirt, and a separate pleated standing collar. The woman who chose these embellishments understood how a contrast of color would create interest and highlight the garment's lines with steel blue bias strips edging the collar's knife pleats, skirt details, and cuff trim. Thick blue piping finishes both collar and bodice hems, while embroidered buttons close the bodice. The dress has contrasting texture in its ribbed faille fabric and silk satin trim strategically accented with fringe, which creates movement when worn. Victorian fashion was not for the well-to-do alone, it was for anyone who could sew.

FIG. 11. *Four different edge treatments, contrasting colors and textures, pleats and ruffles, and more make this gown much more complex than it seems at first. See Plate 1 (p. 4).*

Plate 2
Architectural Beauty and the Brown Decades

c. 1880
Silk, satin and taffeta

R eading like a page taken from a Victorian architectural pattern book, this striking two-piece walking dress offers surprises from every vantage point. The pattern book effect is especially true of the elaborate overdress, where no two views are the same and where pleats, scallops, ruching, appliqué and ruffles are all displayed. The key to the visual richness is the use of fabrics whose tones match even as their textures contrast. This dress, echoing the colors of New York and Boston brownstone townhouses of the era, has a lustrous sheen due to its fabrics and would have announced the arrival of its wearer through its gentle rustling sweep.

Asymmetry is built into the very design of the garment with its array of embellishments. False turnbacks at the deliberately irregular overskirt hem are appliquéd to look as though the lining is being revealed. One side of the dress is almost plain, with a simple ruche capturing the fabric and allowing it to flow toward the bustle, anchored with a contrasting appliqué panel. Intricate layers of trim cover the other side of the skirt with rows of tile-like scallops—strikingly similar to the fish-scale slate roof tiles seen on High Victorian Gothic buildings, such as Memorial Hall at Harvard University. Scallops of an entirely different shape finish the underskirt and train, echoing a Victorian Gothic colonnade. Like a musical score, each element builds on the other to reach a crescendo. Cut in smooth flowing lines over the hips, this dress has the low, unsupported pouf-like bustle of the early 1880s, before the emergence of exaggerated, structurally supported bustles later in the decade.

Bowen Collection, University Museum, Accession No. 57
See also Figs. 6, 12, 13, 14, 15, 38, 80, 81, 82, 83, 127,
140

FIG. 12. *Asymmetrical cuff with contrasting textures.*

FIG. 13. *Skirt trim with dags pointing in opposite directions.*

Asymmetry

Though fashionable only for a relatively short time toward the end of the nineteenth century, asymmetry in clothing is a playful aspect of garment design.

Asymmetry is a major design element for the gown in Plate 2 (p. 10), where every embellishment on the garment is asymmetrical except for the bodice. The dress is described in detail in Plate 2, however these close-up images allow in-depth examination. The appliquéd cuffs, for example, deliberately extend one side higher than the other (fig. 12). The left side of the overskirt skirt has rows of geometrical dagged shapes pointing downward, while the right side of the overskirt has the same shapes appliquéd in place pointing up (fig. 13). This one garment has examples of almost every concept discussed in this book, but the characteristic that makes it all work as a cohesive design is the asymmetry. It becomes the framework for what would otherwise be chaotic.

For example, asymmetry allows the overskirt to become a series of impressions flowing into each other. The hem is constructed on a dynamic diagonal. Above it, the fabric sweeps across the skirt from right to left, released from a long, anchoring appliqué of smooth, piped silk running down the right side, creating a visually rich gathered area in the front that is pulled together into a broad vertical ruffled band down the left side (fig. 14). The fabric emerges from the ruffle into a very formal arrangement of pleat and scallop bands that define the left side of the skirt, and these suddenly give way to softly gathered, unstructured fabric toward the back. This is pulled into a low bustle creating a swoop to one side rather than the usual even, centered pouf (fig. 15), which in turn is pleated into several large, deep knife pleats before reaching around to the right side front and back into the anchoring appliqué band. It is a breathtaking dress, and it owes much of its impact to asymmetry; it is impossible to appreciate it from a single angle and requires a 360-degree viewing to fully experience it. The garment would have presented a continually shifting impression as the wearer moved.

FIG. 14. *Overskirt treatment with asymmetrical tailoring.*

FIG. 15. *Asymmetrical bustle sweeping to the right.*

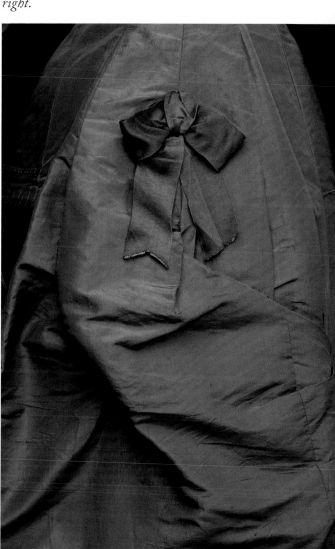

Before they considered even an inch of trim, Victorian designers imagined the lush effects possible simply by using the color, texture, and composition of the fabric at hand. This way of thinking about design can be found to one degree or another in dresses from all walks of life and over the entire era, and is evident in the approach to the construction of trimmings.

But how were these trims and embellishments originally made? How can they be replicated? The next portion of the book examines specific techniques and "goes under the hood" for a maker's view of construction. The following techniques build on the principles previously discussed in this chapter:

Ruching
Pleating
Ribbon work
Bound edges
Piping
Cord and braid work
Appliqué
Passementerie

Instructions are derived from a close hands-on examination of the garments, taking advantage of places where threads have loosened to peer at the back side of pleat bands, searching garment interiors for cording ends, and studying fabric grain lines and seams for clues to construction. Basic sewing skills are assumed in the instructions, although appendices in the back have stitch diagrams and a glossary of terms.

Alternate view of Plate 2 (p. 10)

FIG. 16. *Detail of ruching at hem, see Plate 3 (p. 18).*

FIG. 17. Godey's *1869, with a three-part trim featuring ruching at the center of a box-pleated element.*

Key

right side of fabric #1

wrong side of fabric #1

right side of fabric #2

wrong side of fabric #2

■ ■ ■ ■ ■ ■ stitch line

● ● ● ● ● ● ● fold line

2

Ruching

There is some confusion in nineteenth-century manuals and fashion descriptions between ruching and pleating, the terms are often used interchangeably. For the purposes of this book, ruching refers to a soft gathered fabric treatment, while pleats are measured pressed folds of fabric.

Applied ruching in this era was created on a separate strip of fabric that was then applied as trim. It can be seen as part of a more complex trim such as in figure 16, where the ruching strip is applied to the top of a band of knife pleats, hiding the stitch line attaching the pleats to the skirt. This kind of ruching is the most basic: raw edges of a strip of fabric are pressed to the back, a running stitch is sewn along top and bottom, and then pulled taut to gather the fabric slightly. The ruching strip is sewn to the garment, securing it without losing the softness of the gathered fabric, yet firmly enough to prevent it from catching on things in passing.

Ruching can also take on more complex forms. A fashion plate from *Godey's Lady's Book* in 1869 shows an example, with a ruched band of repeating poufs set on top of a wider box pleated strip (fig. 17). The poufs are made from a fabric strip sewn into a tube, which is then further manipulated with vertical gathering stitches every few inches. A band of fabric is then wrapped around the pinched-in areas of the poufs, making an elaborate three-part trim.

Plate 3
The All Important Silhouette: Daisy's Cherry Day Dress

c. early 1880s
Wool twill and silk satin ribbon

This bright, cheery, cherry wool day dress is a charming garment in fine condition. Its flattering darts run over the bust and flow past the hips, creating the long visual line known as a princess cut. This style was popularized in the early 1880s by Alexandra, Princess of Wales (1844–1925), Queen Victoria's daughter-in-law and fashion trendsetter.

As with the dress in Plate 1 (p. 4), this is a homemade effort. The seamstress used her sewing machine wisely; the dress is a practical combination of hand and machine stitching. Rows of pleating and ruching make this practical wool dress a charming choice for everyday use inside the home or for daytime excursions. The trims are cut from the same fine cherry wool fabric as the dress itself, with occasional accents of silk ribbons. Two different fabric strips manipulated independently are sewn together to make the trims: most are knife pleats edged on one side with a narrower box-pleated strip, and a variant at the hem is made with a wider knife pleat band paired with a strip of ruched fabric.

There are twelve yards of fabric in the knife pleats alone on this dress, all requiring tedious hemming. The seamstress displayed ingenuity here—the hemming is done quickly by machine, and with the hems deliberately turned to the outside to create the extra effect of edge binding. Adding to the overall cohesion of the gown are the buttons, which, in combination with the bright color, would have captured the gaze of those in the drawing room or passersby on a city stroll.

Note: The dress was given to the Bowen collection by Daisy Dean Williamson, a Cooperative Extension instructor between 1920 and 1942. There is no information on whether this dress was acquired over the course of her travels or whether it was an heirloom left to her by her mother, Martha Alldredge Williamson, who would have been the right age to wear the dress as a young woman. A noted collector of paisley shawls, Ms. Williamson bequeathed one hundred and sixty of them to the University of New Hampshire.

Bowen Collection, University Museum, Accession No. 31,
Gift of Daisy Deane Williamson
See also Figs. 1, 16, 37, 42, 48, 49

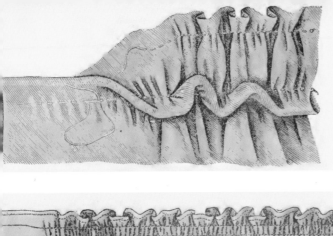

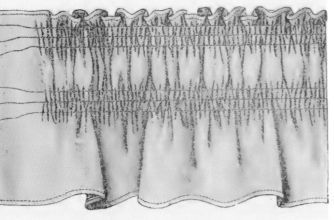

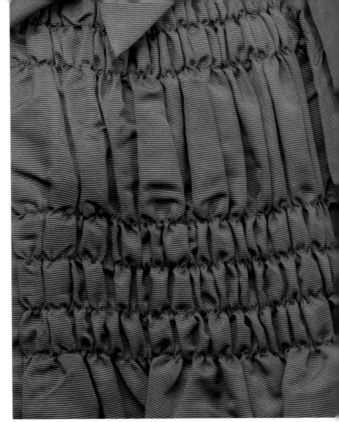

FIG. 19. *Four short rows of ruching in two sets, see Plate 4 (p. 24).*

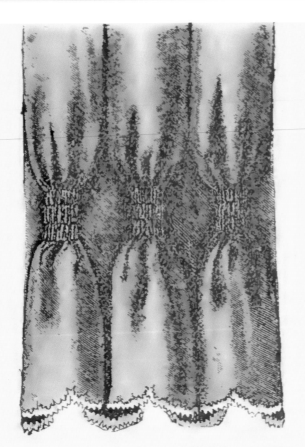

FIG. 18A–C. *A few* Hecklinger's, *variants on how to add interest to a ruched band.*

There are hundreds of variations on ruching described at length in many popular women's journals and how-to guides. These journals were found in households regardless of economic level. One such example is *Hecklinger's Ladies' Garments*, a sewing manual published in 1886 (fig. 18a-c), with examples shown here.

Some forms of ruching can be done in the middle of a dress, as a way of gathering excess fabric, controlling it, and adding visual interest. The short lines of ruching at the top left of the skirt shown in figure 19 are an isolated accent—all the remaining embellishments on the suit (Plate 4, p. 24) are pleated. Clearly, this was meant to stand out!

Making Basic (Horizontal) Ruching

Materials & Supplies:
fabric (matching or contrasting the garment)
needle
thread

These basic instructions will produce ruching like that used in figure 16; once you have the basic concept down, explore the variations.

FIG. 20

FIG. 21

1.) Cut a strip of fabric, either on the straight grain or on the bias, depending your desired effect. Turn the raw edges under at top and bottom (fig. 20).

Knot the thread. Make regular small running stitches along the top of the strip, capturing both the front and the folded under fabric. Repeat for the bottom (fig. 21).

FIG. 22

3.) Holding one end firmly in one hand, grasp the top and bottom thread together in the other and pull gently against the knots. The fabric will slide down the threads and it can be bunched as much or as little as desired. Tie off the threads once satisfied that the gathers will stay put (fig. 22).

4.) Arrange the strip on the garment. Tuck the short raw end to the back. Pin in place every few inches. At the opposite end, tuck the short raw end under. Hand stitch in place along the top and bottom with whipstitches, making sure to attach the ruching firmly without big gaps, but without collapsing the fullness. Figure 23 from *Hecklinger's* demonstrates this method.

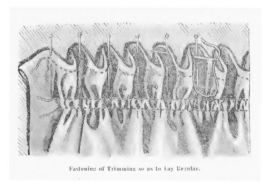

Fastening of Trimming so as to lay Regular.

FIG. 23

RUCHING

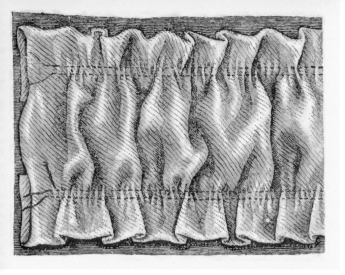

FIG. 24

Hecklinger's directions for ruching consist of an image and no descriptive text (fig. 24). Visually, there is a lot of information here. This particular variation is not hemmed first, rather the raw edges are turned to the back so that the gathering stitches secure them in place. Gathering is achieved by placing a double row of fairly small running stitches at the top and bottom of the fabric strip. Evenly slide the fabric along the taut thread to form the gathers.

Making Godey's *Vertical Ruching* (fig. 17)

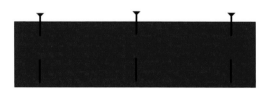

FIG. 25

FIG. 26

1.) Repeat Step 1 (p. 21), OR take the fabric and sew it into a long tube and turn it right side out, capturing both raw long edges inside.

2.) Decide how tightly to space the poufs. Determine the spacing, add ¼″ to account for shrinkage when gathering and mark with pins for the whole length of your strip (fig. 25).

3.) Knot the thread, beginning and ending from the back, and take three or four running stitches vertically through both layers of fabric from one edge to the other. Pull tight, gathering into a pouf. Anchor the thread. Repeat for the next pouf (fig. 26).

4.) Attach to the garment as in Step 4 on page 21, stitching down at every vertical gather (fig. 23). To wrap a ribbon around as in the *Godey's* example (fig. 17), do so before stitching to the garment. To start and finish, tuck the raw short ends under at one of the vertical gathers and secure to the garment.

5.) If the ruching strip is not long enough, make another and butt it up against the one already sewn down. The "join" should disappear visually because of the gathers. (fig. 27).

FIG. 27

Making Ruched Zones in Garments *(fig. 19)*

The following instructions explain the technique used on the suit illustrated in Plate 4 (p. 24).

FIG. 28

1.) This can be done either to a finished garment or to the fabric before it is assembled. Decide where to place the rows of ruching, how tightly to pull the ruching (the tighter, the more fabric it will gather), the number of rows desired, and how they should be spaced. Mark the beginning and end of each line of stitching with pins (fig. 28).

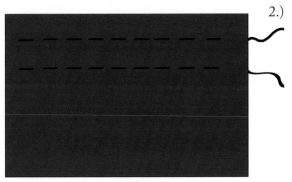

FIG. 29

2.) Either with machine basting stitches or by hand with regular running stitches, sew from a start point to a finish point for each line of gathering. Begin and end at the back of the ruching piece so the knots and loose ends are on the reverse and not visible when the work is completed. Remove pins (fig. 29).

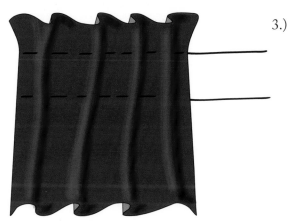

FIG. 30

3.) Holding the fabric and threads firmly on one side, gently pull on the threads from the other end to evenly distribute the fabric into gathers along the length of the thread (if by hand, pull on the thread; if by machine, then pull on the surface thread). Tie off on the inside when the desired length is reached (fig. 30).

Plate 4
The Victorian Wedding Palette vs. White Wedding Gowns:
Johanna Peterson's Dress

c. 1890
Silk faille

This claret asymmetrical dress is beautifully crafted and tailored, with a false jacket over an intricately pleated shell made with four distinct layers closed by 14 buttons and 33 hooks and eyes. The sleeves have a distinctive pleated embellishment sewn into the shoulders and cuffs, and the skirt is accented with knife pleats made especially crisp by the ribbed silk faille fabric of the dress, and asymmetrical off center soft ruching just at one hip. All the embellishments are made by folding and manipulating the fabric of the dress itself, there is not one piece of extra trim or decoration aside from a bit of lace at the cuffs.

Family history suggests that this petite garment was the wedding dress of Johanna Peterson, who married Jens Peterson in Bedford, Massachusetts, in 1893, three years after Johanna emigrated to the United States from Denmark. Although contemporary taste suggests that white, cream, and ivories are "appropriate" colors for wedding gowns, the Victorian palette was wider ranging, frequently employing darker hues such as olive green, bronze brown, gray and mauve, depending on the style and season. In addition, not every bride could afford a white dress to be worn for just one occasion and so this falls under the category of Best Dress to be worn again later, rather than the classic single-use white bridal gown. Nonetheless it was stylish and would have projected confidence as Johanna took on a new role in society and in her new home. The Petersons became a classic American immigrant's success story: grandson Walter J. Peterson became a college president and the 72nd governor of the state of New Hampshire.

Bowen Collection, University Museum, Accession No. 2000.1,
Gift of Dorothy and Walter J. Peterson Jr.
See also Figs. 19, 31, 61, 62

FIG. 31. *Close up of pleated cuff, see Plate 4 (p. 24).*

3

Pleats

Pleats are ubiquitous in Victorian design, found on trim bands (Plate 2, p. 10), elaborate skirt ruffles (Plate 6, p. 56), and even carefully sculptured cuffs (fig. 31). As complex as they may appear to be, decorative pleats belong to one of two main families: knife pleats and box pleats. Both knife and box pleats can be made as a single repeat, or in more complex patterns where pleats are stacked numerous times before moving on to form another pleat grouping in the design (fig. 32). A pleat pattern can be made using only one kind of pleat, but knife and box pleats can also be used in combination with each other for more elaborate effect (fig. 46).

General Guidelines on All Pleats

Regardless of the type of pleating to be used, certain guidelines apply across the board.

1.) Determining fabric quantity is key, pleats take up a lot of fabric. Measure the desired finished length (i.e. a skirt hem) and multiply as follows:

Single pleats = finished length x 3
Double stacked pleats = finished length x 5
Triple stacked pleats = finished length x 7

2.) Decide how to finish the edges before pleating. Edges can be hemmed with a ¼″ rolled hem, cut with pinking shears, wrapped with a bias binding (figs. 92-95), or enclosed within a tube as with figure 17. All are perfectly acceptable solutions.

3.) Use a steam iron to press the pleats in place, or they will not hold their crisp shape. Iron with an up and down (vertical) motion, not a back and forth (horizontal) motion, which will distort the fabric. *Always test on a scrap of the fabric first.*

FIG. 32. *Edge view of double box pleats on a silk skirt, Accession No. 76.2. See Figs. 56 and 57 for additional views.*

FIG. 33

Knife Pleats

Knife pleats are the simplest form of pleating. The fabric is folded continually in one direction in a zigzag pattern (fig. 33). In describing pleats, all folds made upward are peak folds, and all folds made downward are valley folds.

Making Knife Pleats

Materials & supplies:

    fabric for pleating, with finished edges
    chalk for marking (optional)
    pins
    ruler
    needle or sewing machine
    thread
    steam iron
    press cloth
    vinegar solution

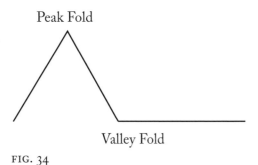

Peak Fold

Valley Fold

FIG. 34

1.) Knife pleats are built on a 3:1 ratio; three inches of fabric will create one inch of finished pleats. For example, for a finished inch of pleats that show on the surface for ½″, the fabric will need to have a peak fold at 1″, a valley fold at ½″, a peak fold at 1″, a valley fold at ½″, etc. This will create two pleats in a one inch space. The fabric can be marked with chalk or with pins; mark before pleating (fig. 35). Depending on your design, you can of course choose to make shallower pleats that use less fabric.

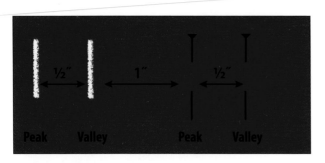

FIG. 35

2.) Start with a peak fold at the first pin and a valley fold at the second pin. The peak fold should then fall halfway to the next mark. Crease the fabric, remove marking pins, and set another pin in the pleat to keep it in place. Repeat till the strip is completed. (fig. 36)

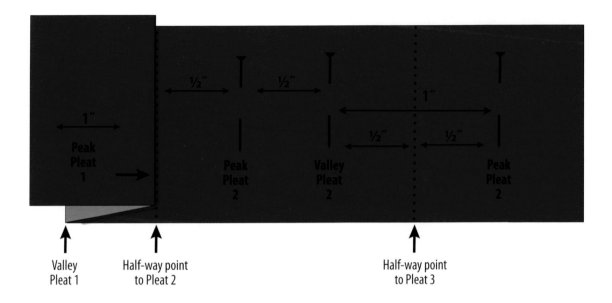

FIG. 36

3.) Press to help set the creases. Remove pins.

TIP:
Mix one part water to one part white distilled vinegar and dampen a press cloth with this solution. Press with as hot an iron as the fabric can safely handle until the press cloth is dry. Do not move your pleated fabric until it has cooled completely. This will set the pleat as little else will! This technique can be used to remove old creases too. Always test on a scrap first!

You can use your knife pleat bands in a variety of ways to create many different effects. They can be attached only at the top, which allows them to fan fully at the hem like a ruffle (fig. 37). If more control is needed, additional tacking stitches can be done invisibly from behind to tack down the band here and there and keep it from flipping up.

FIG. 37. *Knife-pleated trim attached only at the top by hand, flipped up in the photograph to show the stitches. See Plate 3 (p. 18).*

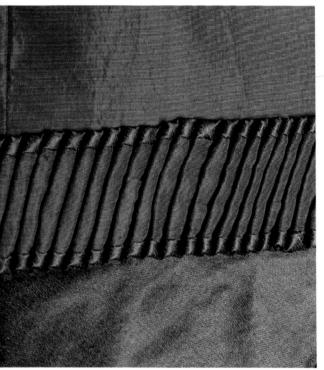

Knife pleats also can be sewn down at both top and bottom to form a completely controlled band. The band in figure 38 has additional manipulations in that the pleats have had their raw edges bound with a strip of bias fabric (see chapter 5) and have then been pulled to the diagonal and set.

To do this, cut your strip of fabric on the straight grain and sew bias binding to the edges. Make knife pleats, and press lightly. Then, using pins, anchor the top edge to your press board or ironing board and firmly pull the bottom edge to one side. The fabric has enough elasticity to shift the pleat pattern over while maintaining the straight grain. Press well, preferably with the vinegar solution.

FIG. 38. *Trim band made with a simple knife pleat, edged with bias binding, given a little extra visual power by stretching to a slight angle. See Plate 2 (p. 10).*

There is plenty of opportunity for creativity even with this simple knife pleat variant. Figure 39 shows a pleated band with bias binding tacking down both sides, but the knife pleat has been given a twist so that pleats are pointing down on the right and up on the left. In this example the sheen of the silk satin gives the twisted pleats an extra visual dimension, and the pleats are not pressed and crisp but rather left soft so as to accentuate the torque and catch the light.

FIG. 39. *Close up of a trim band made of a twisted knife pleat, day dress from early 1870s, silk taffeta, Accession No. 29.*

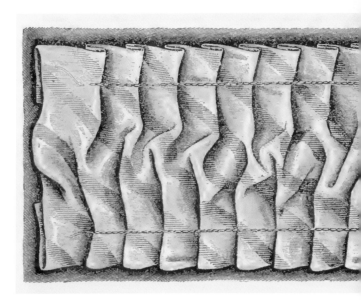

FIG. 40

Hecklinger's explanation of how to create the twisted knife pleat used in figure 39 is just a simple line drawing (fig. 40). This variation does not seal the edges in a bias binding, but rather turns the raw edges to the back.

FIG. 41

Box Pleats

Box pleats can be thought of as mirrored knife pleats with alternating folds (fig. 41). They can be spaced so that the folds all touch, or further apart so that the trim becomes an alternating pattern (fig. 42). Box pleated trims are versatile (fig. 43). They can be attached near the top of the band to create a ruffle with a frilled head, stitched along the middle to form fabric ruffles evenly spaced from the top and bottom, or evenly sewn at top and bottom to make a firm textured band.

These pleats can also be inverted, so that the box-like shape is to the back, although this really only shows if the pleats are spaced apart. Also box pleats can be stacked to further manipulate the fabric (figs. 56, 57).

FIG. 42. *Detail, of Plate 3 (p. 18), with trim made of spaced out box pleats.*

The details in figure 43 show box pleat trims on a gown from the late 1850s. The first photograph illustrates box pleats sewn to the garment both at top and bottom of the pleated trim band (fig. 43a). The effect is to create a solid but textured trim, in this case at the hem of the skirt. The second photograph illustrates two types of attachment (fig. 43b) with one type of band sewn to the gown sleeves near the top of the pleats and the others sewn to the gown's bodice in the middle of the trim. By altering the placement of the attachment stitching, the same style of band produces two different frill effects. This one dress is decorated solely with box pleats, but achieves three distinct trims.

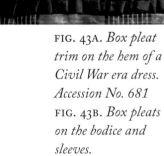

FIG. 43A. *Box pleat trim on the hem of a Civil War era dress. Accession No. 681*
FIG. 43B. *Box pleats on the bodice and sleeves.*

Making Box Pleats

Materials & supplies:
- fabric with finished edges
- chalk for marking (optional)
- pins
- ruler
- needle or sewing machine
- thread
- steam iron
- press cloth
- vinegar solution

1.) As with knife pleats, box pleats are built on a 3:1 ratio; three inches of fabric create one inch of finished pleats. To make a finished inch of pleating composed of two regularly spaced ½″ box pleats, the fabric will need to have a valley fold at ½″, a peak fold at ¼″, a peak fold at ½″, a valley fold at ¼″, a valley fold at ½″, a peak fold at ¼″ a peak fold at ½″ and a valley at ¼″, etc. The fabric can be marked with chalk or with pins; mark before pleating (fig. 44).

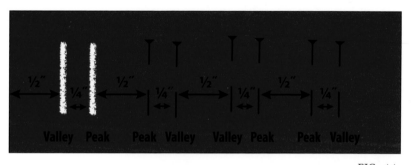

FIG. 44

2.) Begin with a valley fold at the first pin and a peak fold at the second pin. The peak fold should fall back to the left. To complete the box, make another peak fold at the next pin and a valley at the pin after that. This peak fold should fall to the right, and the folds of the smaller pleats should touch behind the middle of the surface pleat. Crease the fabric, remove marking pins, and set pins in the pleats to keep them in place. Repeat until the strip is completed (fig. 45).

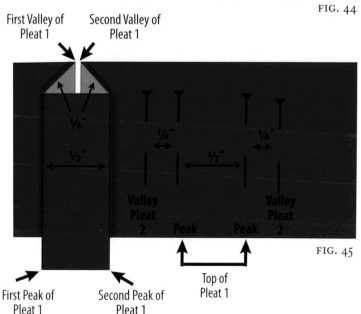

FIG. 45

3.) Press with a steam iron while using a press cloth moistened with the water and vinegar solution to help set the creases. Remove pins.

Pleat Combinations

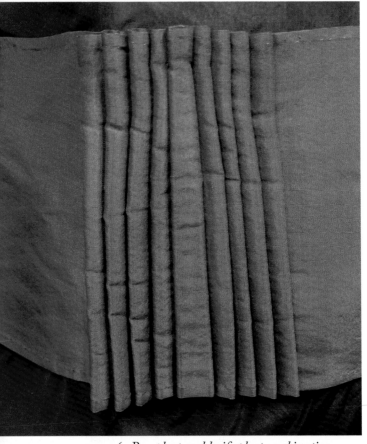

Victorian designers often played with pleat combinations, either as built-up bands or by spacing and combining pleats onto one piece of fabric. Here are several examples. Figure 46 illustrates a grouping made of one box pleat flanked on either side by four knife pleats, then a plain section of trim. This pattern is repeated and eventually forms a band used as skirt trim. As applied, only the top edge of the trim is attached to the dress, the bottom edge is finished by hand with a tiny turned-under hem. Figure 47 diagrams the pattern, and in this example each stack of pleats as defined by the dashed lines takes 7½˝.

FIG. 46. *Box pleat and knife pleat combination for gown in Plate 6 (p. 56).*
Below: Pleat diagram for this treatment.

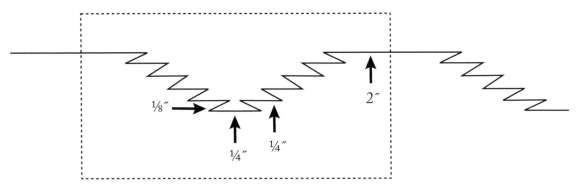

FIG. 47 *Pleat diagram for above treatment.*

Figure 48 is an example of a multiple-part trim, where two distinct, individually finished pleat strips have been combined to create one intricate trim. The narrow strip of box pleats overlays the top of the knife pleat trim. The knife pleat trim is hemmed to the front by machine along one edge and the other, unfinished edge is hand stitched to the dress, letting the finished edge flare free. Both edges of the box pleats are machine hemmed to the front, and the pleats themselves are held in place with a machine stitch running through the center. They are then applied to the gown by hand with basting stitches along that same center stitch line, allowing the box pleats to flare evenly.

The dress uses a similar technique at the hem, only here the knife pleated band is topped with a ruched border piece (fig. 49).

Note: It appears that the maker was not terribly careful; in some places the pleat strip was hemmed to the front, and in others it was flipped over and hemmed to the back.

FIG. 48. *Combination box pleats and knife pleats trimming gown in Plate 3 (p. 18).*

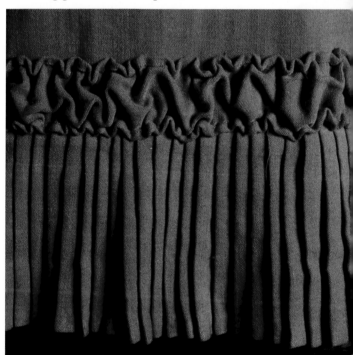

FIG. 49. *Ruching combined with knife pleats on the hem of the skirt.*

Sculptural Pleats

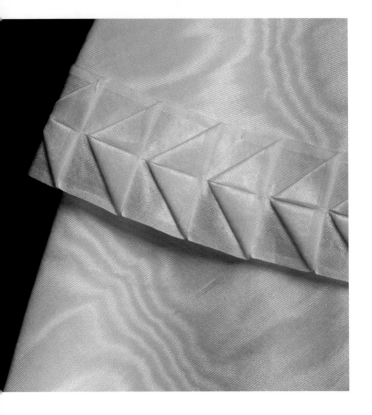

Both knife and box pleats lend themselves to elaboration. The Victorians loved taking these basic folds and amplifying them with additional manipulation. A simple example is illustrated by figures 50a-b, a striking trim created by taking a regular knife pleat and folding down the corners to create dynamic arrows. In this case the trim is a ribbon rather than a finished strip of fabric and the arrows are pressed into position after folding. See figure 64 for additional ways to enhance this pleat.

FIG. 50A. *Detail of trim on silk jacket c. 1850, Accession No. 71. Series of knife pleats folded into arrows.*

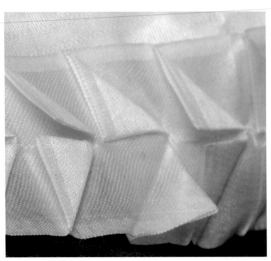

FIG. 50B

FIG. 50B *shows a close up of the crease from a partially unfolded arrow.*

Box pleats can also be modified in a number of ways. A common example is illustrated by figure 51. The center of each box pleat edge is brought up to meet in the middle forming two triangles or one diamond shaped detail on top and below. This is a "squash fold" in origami. In this example an additional decorative band passes through the middle of the box pleat around which the diamond shapes are folded.

The pleat is made as follows:

1.) Make a box pleat twice as high as it is wide (fig. 52).

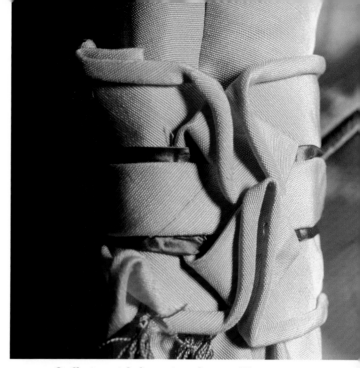

FIG. 51. *Cuff trim with decorative pleat, see Plate 1 (p. 4).*

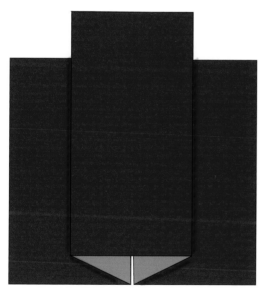

FIG. 52

2.) Pull the center of the bottom half of the pleat (D) up to meet the middle of the pleat (C). The fabric will make a new corner at the middle of the bottom half of the pleat (A) (fig. 53).

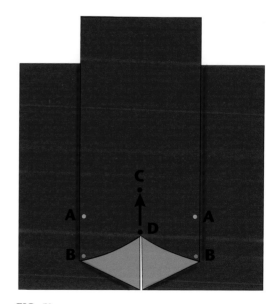

FIG. 53

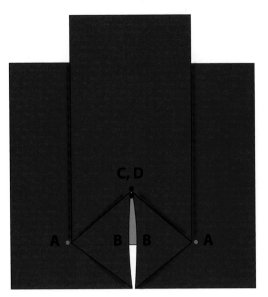

FIG. 54

3.) The left and right points (B) that used to be on the bottom edge of the pleat at the original box folds now meet parallel to points (A) (fig. 54).

FIG. 55

There are many variations on this idea. This trim illustrated in *Hecklinger's* (fig. 55) shows box pleats that have a little tuck made toward the top of the pleat, where the box pleat is stitched to the garment, by bringing the peak fold on the right over to the one on the left. The top section is folded into a triangular shape reminiscent of the example shown in figure 51.

FIG. 56. *Stacked box pleats on a silk skirt,*
Accession No. 76.2.

FIG. 57. *View of the additional squash fold.*
Accession No. 76.2.

Figures 56 and 57 are alternate views of figure 32. The silk skirt has self trim at the hem made of a double-stacked box pleat. This is a classic example—two pleats constructed on top of each other as the diagram shows (fig. 58)—then machine stitched across the middle.

The same fold as in figure 51 gives the top layer an extra flourish.

In the sample diagram (fig. 58), each stack of pleats as defined by the dashed lines takes 5 inches, and the three pleats shown take 15 inches total.

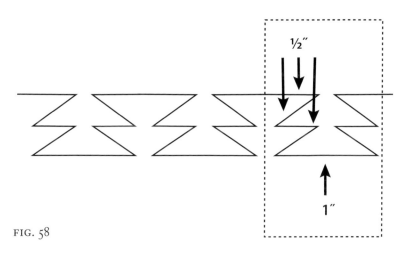

FIG. 58

Hecklinger's sample of a triple box pleat pattern shows pleats that are not stacked directly on top of each other but rather incrementally widen on each side of the center pleat until an inverted (inside out) box pleat is formed between each triple pleat unit (fig. 59). This is done by having the return not meet in the center of the top pleat. The diagram illustrated in figure 60 shows another view. With the sample measurements given, each set of pleats as defined by the dashed lines takes 3¼″ and the entire diagram as shown takes 11½″.

This is similar to the knife and box pleat combination of figures 46 and 47, but because it is so densely folded and feeds directly into the next repeat with no space, it really is more of a triple box pleat than a combination pleat.

FIG. 59

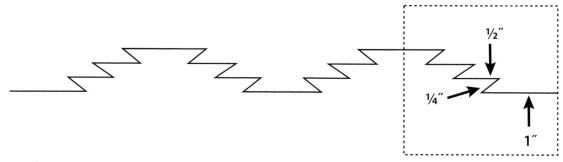

FIG. 60

Not all pleating trims are in bands. The suit in Plate 4 (p. 24) has sleeves with a puffed shoulder head added as a self-contained element after the main sleeve construction (fig. 61). Dress fabric is pleated into the shoulder seam of the finished sleeve and allowed to softly puff before being tacked into a crisply defined box pleat flanked by three inward-pointing knife pleats at the bicep. These pleats are drawn into a narrowing shape by overlapping them more tightly toward the elbow, until the fabric is finished with a knot and tacked to the sleeve (fig. 62). Figure 63 is a schematic diagram of the folds but is not to scale. The proportions depend entirely on the size of the sleeve being made and the knot should fall about three inches above the elbow.

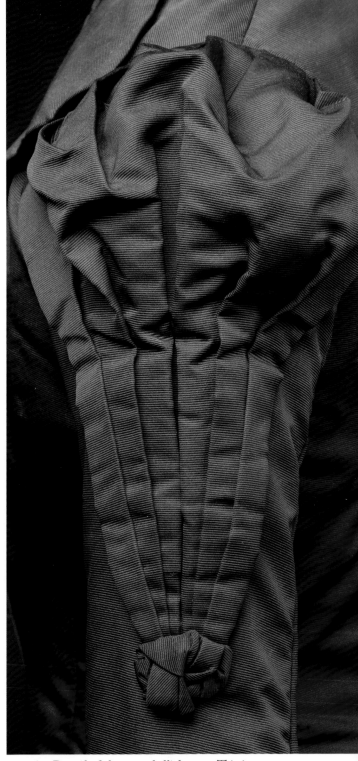

FIG. 61. *Detail of sleeve embellishment. This is a completely finished element added to the finished sleeve. See Plate 4 (p. 24).*

FIG. 62. *Close view of the knot. The pleated fabric is manipulated into a twist that hides its raw end.*

FIG. 63

14″ of fabric including seam allowance before pleating down to the shoulder of the finished sleeve.

| peak fold
• valley fold

Area between the pleats is loosely folded.

Sharply defined knife pleats necking down at stitch line.

Narrowed pleats folded into a knot.

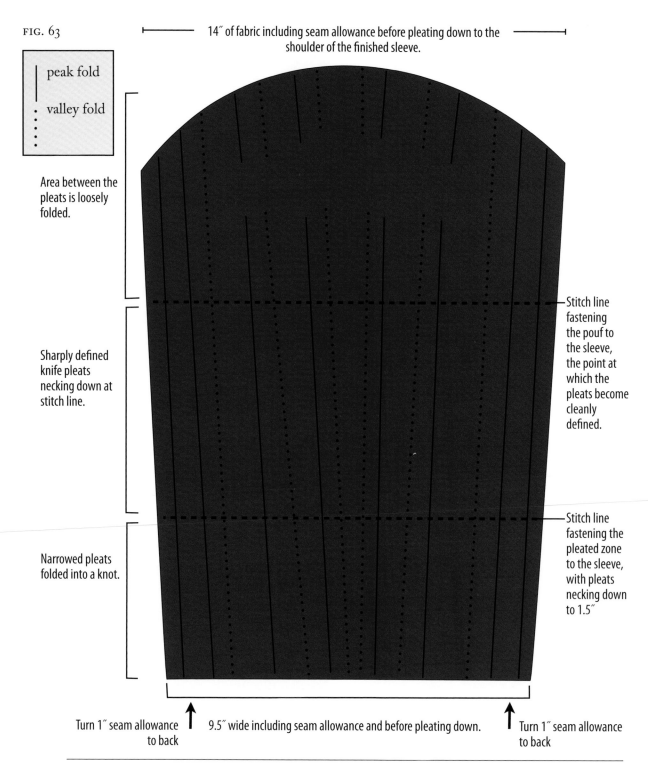

Stitch line fastening the pouf to the sleeve, the point at which the pleats become cleanly defined.

Stitch line fastening the pleated zone to the sleeve, with pleats necking down to 1.5″

Turn 1″ seam allowance to back

9.5″ wide including seam allowance and before pleating down.

Turn 1″ seam allowance to back

The distance from the top of the shoulder to the knot is 8.5″, and the knot itself is 1.25″ wide.

Diagram of pleat structure at first stitch line; pleats do not overlap.

Diagram of pleat structure right above the knot, with deeply overlapping pleats.

Plate 5
Haute Couture Arrives in America: Maison Rouff Tea Gown

c. 1900
Design, Maison Rouff, Paris
Wool, silk satin ribbons, silk cord, silk net, lace

Maison Rouff was one of the leading design houses of Paris in the late nineteenth century, a contemporary of Frederick Worth and Emile Pingat. *Harper's Bazar*, catering to fashion-conscious middle and upper class American women as early as 1867, frequently featured Paris gowns in its pages, and Maison Rouff's offerings could be found among them. The house was known for its elaborate day dresses and was a destination for wealthy American ladies seeking to treat themselves to the lavish shopping experience, extraordinary fit, and attention to detail of haute couture—and dazzle society back home with their Parisian wardrobes.

The sumptuous light weight wool gown has a full skirt with a train covered in silk roses and vine-like fronds and cord. The embellishments are especially fine and offer numerous opportunities for adaptation to current garment design. Panels of mesh highlight the waist and a delicate net finishes the bodice, sleeves, and high collar. The lower portion of the sleeves is missing.

Note: It is likely that this stunning example from Maison Rouff is a tea gown. An extraordinarily similar garment in the collection of Kent State University (Accession No. 1983. 001.0289) has the identical skirt but a bodice finished with different lace fall and sleeves—one can picture well-to-do American ladies perusing fashion plate samples, choosing this skirt but that bodice, this lace but that sleeve.

Bowen Collection, University Museum, Accession No. 177
See also figures 10, 64, 66, 72, 73, 112, 117

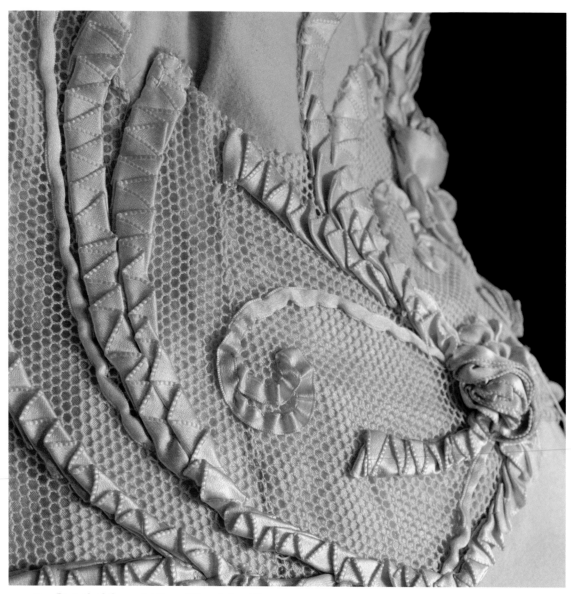

FIG. 64. *Detail of the waist from Plate 5 (p. 44).*

4

Ribbon Work

Victorian women's journals are full of tips and tricks for ribbon work, as well as ways to apply these trims and decorations to every imaginable surface (fig. 65). Many of these techniques rely on the same kind of single and stacked pleats already discussed in Chapter 3, as well as additional manipulations such as in figures 50 and 51. This form of embellishment was one anyone could try with a bit of ribbon, a needle, and some thread, but it was found on high-end garments as well, such as the gown in Plate 5 (p. 44). The intricate ribbon fronds and roses on this Maison Rouff gown were applied by hand in a Parisian haute couture workshop. Figure 64 shows the interplay between techniques, with the ribbons worked into flowing shapes punctuated by lush roses—both decorating the gown and forming a transition between the wool and net areas of the dress. This chapter focuses on the two distinct frond styles used here by the Maison Rouff seamstresses.

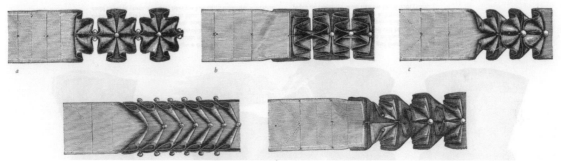

FIG. 65. *Ribbon trims from* Godey's Lady's Book, *1867*

Making Two Parisian Fronds

FIG. 66. *The beginning of the large frond on the bottom is covered by the narrow frond on the top.*

Materials & Supplies:

double-faced satin ribbon, preferably silk
(thick, synthetic ribbon is harder to
work with)
embroidery hoop for small projects or
needlework frame for large ones
pins
needle
thread

For both fronds:

1.) Determine the design. Be prepared for it to
shift a little while working, as this is a very
organic technique. How the ribbon feels while
working it will help determine the placement.
The design can be drawn onto fabric with
chalk or you can make guidelines with basting
stitches. For more complex designs, see the
Appendix for tips on transferring patterns to
fabric.

2.) Stretch the fabric gently over a hoop or frame.

3.) Fold the very tip of the ribbon to the back
to contain fraying or apply an optional fray
preventative like Fray Check™. Pin in place
to anchor the work. The beginning of each
frond can be hidden by another element in
your design (fig. 66).

Frond Type 1: Pleated

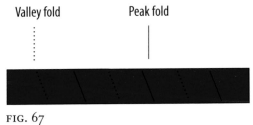

Valley fold   Peak fold

FIG. 67

1.) The basic manipulation of the ribbon is to fold it back and forth on itself in a zigzag, and to tack it in place at each turning. Figure 67 shows the fold pattern with the ribbon flat.

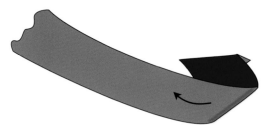

FIG. 68

2.) You are working the frond from its wider end down toward the narrower base where it joins the overall design. Tuck the raw end under and pin, then fold the ribbon over. Anchor the new crease with a pin (fig. 68).

FIG. 69

3.) Fold the ribbon over the frond to form the first segment that hides the start of the ribbon. Pin in place (fig. 69)

4.) Continue folding over. Pin each in place. Figure 70 shows the next three folds in sequence.

FIG. 70

> **TIP:**
> As you get comfortable with this technique you may end up stitching the ribbon down as your frond grows instead of pinning, but for now as you learn to adjust your curves, shapes, and pleat density, use your pins.

FIG. 71

5.) Experiment with how tight the zigzags need to be to get the desired shape. Shallow pleats will create a wider frond, stretched-out pleats will make the frond narrower. Slowly increase the steepness of the folds to get the ribbon to neck down. Each frond should start wide and grow narrower as it reaches the end (fig. 71).

6.) Try to make sure the inside curve is fairly smooth with the folds of ribbon kept as close to the desired shape as possible. The outside of the curve can be spikier, with the folded corners of the ribbon extending past the line.

7.) At the end of the frond, tuck the cut end of the ribbon under itself or under an adjacent decorative element.

8.) Reposition the pins and curve until satisfied with the shape, then stitch the frond in place with two or three whipstitches at the base of each pleat (fig. 72a). Figure 72b shows how this looks on the actual dress, with arrows pointing to the nearly visible stitches.

FIG. 72A

FIG. 72B

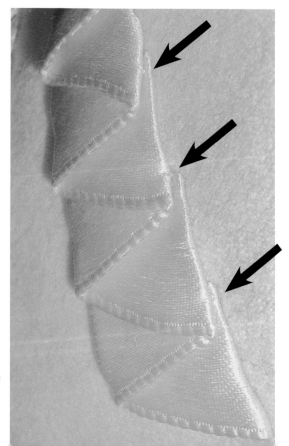

Frond Type 2: Ruched

1.) The second frond type on this dress is a delicate sprig off of the main frond. It uses a much narrower ribbon and is lightly gathered along one edge.

2.) Anchor the base of the frond. Figure 73 illustrates hiding the beginning of the pleated sprig in the frond associated with it.

3.) Using a running stitch, baste with relatively small stitches along the edge that the frond is to curl into. Keep stitches visible from the front small and travel with longer stitches in back (fig. 74).

4.) To curl the ribbon, pull on the basting thread (fig. 75).

5.) Pin into position on the garment.

6.) At the tip of the frond, fold the ribbon back on itself to the inside and tuck a section of it under the surface frond. Make sure the cut end is completely covered by the ribbon on top. The turned-back section should show, creating a deeper frill. Pin to secure.

7.) Using a whipstitch, attach the frond firmly to the garment along both edges at key points, allowing the soft gathers to remain. Where the top ribbon overlaps the bottom ribbon, the unbasted edge can be left free for extra frill effect (fig. 76).

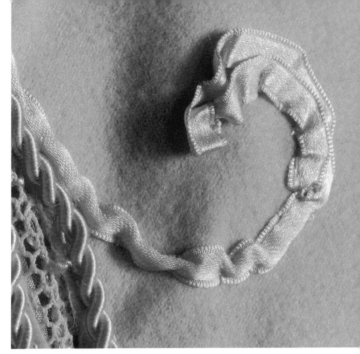

FIG. 73

FIG. 74

FIG. 75

FIG. 76

RIBBON WORK

FIG. 77. *This example is both a contrast in texture (satin strip on ribbed silk) and color (steely blue on ecru), with a pale dress given strong highlights by the edge treatments. See Plate 1 (p. 4).*

5
Bound Edges

Victorian dressmakers often regarded the finishing of hems as an opportunity for additional decoration. Colors or textured fabrics were used to bind raw edges and finish them with a bit of visual punch (fig. 77). In some cases this simple technique turned a plain garment into an outstanding one.

Binding strips are cut on the bias, which is flexible, as fabric cut this way can smoothly follow contours (fig. 78). Unlike modern bias tapes, generally made of poor-quality cottons or polyesters, Victorian bias bindings are rich in color and texture (fig. 79).

In most cases, these bias binding strips are completely finished. Both raw edges of the strip are turned under and stitched down to the garment, enclosing the raw edge of the element being trimmed.

FIG. 78. *Contrast color bias binding following the contours of a bow. This one is machine-applied. See Plate 6 (p. 56).*

FIG. 79. *Bias binding made from blue satin contrast. See Plate 1 (p. 4).*

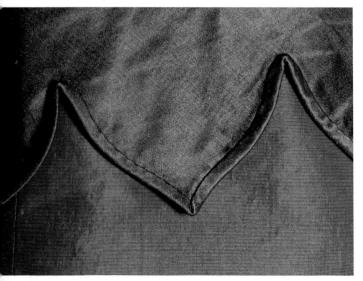

FIG. 80. *Bias binding made from matching fabric, painstakingly applied by hand. See Plate 2.*

Finessing the finishing of shapes can be quite tricky, especially for complex curves, sharp points, or deep incuts. For example, the sharp points and valleys of the shield-shaped scales illustrated in figure 80 required careful pinning and stitching during construction to achieve this clean line. The bias strip and the scales are made of the same fabric and both are cut on the bias, but the bulk of the strip creates a subtle texture effect. Due to the complexity of the shapes the bias strip has been sewn by hand to the front of the scale pattern, then folded over to the back of the scale and finished, also by hand (fig. 81).

FIG. 81. *Underside of the scales. The hand-sewn stitches holding the turned-under raw edge of the bias strip are clearly visible, but do not show on the front.*

Figure 82 is an example from the same garment where a binding strip provides both finish and embellishment, through contrast. A broad strip cut from the same fabric as the dress creates an on-grain ribbon. A contrasting satin-finish textured fabric is used to edge the ribbon prior to pleating; both top and bottom edges on this self-fabric trim piece are edge bound. On this piece of trim, both hand and machine stitches are used. The bias strip is machine sewn to the ribbon by placing right sides together, then folding the raw edge over to the back. As is visible in a small section of trim that has come away slightly from the dress, the raw edge of the bias strip has no further finishing (fig. 83). Next the whole three-part unit is knife pleated, then the pleats offset at a slight angle during pressing. The pleated trim is sewn onto the dress on both the top and bottom, enclosing the raw edges of the bias binding.

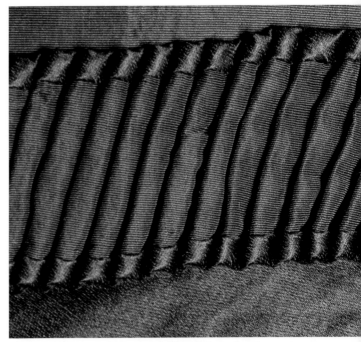

FIG. 82. *The straight grain of the fabric is clearly visible, as is the angled grain of the bias-cut edging. See Plate 2 (p. 10).*

FIG. 83. *The back of the trim was never intended to be exposed, so finishing the inside edges of the bias strips was unnecessary work.*

Plate 6
Structured Elegance: The Stylish Miss Nims

c. 1883
Silk taffeta

This gown came to the collection identified as a Nims family wedding dress, though it could also have been a formal going away dress, a distinction often lost to donors of later generations. The elaborate draping of the skirts in back makes it the height of fashion for 1883, the year Alice Nims married, and the year the bustle re-emerged from its earlier, more softly draped version into this prominent form that would have required a specialized rigid undergarment to support its shape. Whoever wore it would have looked fashionable in the extreme.

The impeccably tailored dress has a bodice flared over the hips, tight sleeves, an underskirt with a slight train, and a draped overskirt gathered into a prominent and iconic mid-1880s bustle. It is notable for its clever treatment of two bronze silk taffetas, each used to trim out the other. Alternating strips of taffeta define the overskirt. Finely knife-pleated rows trim hems and collar. Contrasting narrow bias-cut bands finish the edges of bows, and crisp pleated bands of alternating colors run down the bodice and finish the cuffs. For all the complexity, however, the trims are just basic bias edgings, knife pleats and box pleats—their impact comes from the fact that there are simply quite a lot of them. The dress represents the latest, highest fashion of the day and nothing is out of place or extraneous to the whole, epitomizing the elegance of the era.

The dress has as much visual interest when seen from the back as from the front. It was worn at a time when etiquette suggested that a woman should generally be followed or admired from a respectful distance when in public and any viewer would have been well rewarded with this display, for the skirt has elaborate, bountiful gathering and a lavish bow, all drawing attention to the bustle extending the skirts from the back of the body. To view this dress in profile is also revealing; between the tightly tailored jacket and the rigid bustle, every element of the wearer's movement would have been constrained in some manner and her carriage controlled by her garment.

Note: Sometimes records create more mystery than they solve. Three garments came into the collection from the Nims family: Mary's 1884 high school graduation white cotton shirtwaist, Kate's 1909 blue wool wedding suit (Plate 8, p. 72), and this silk gown, described as matriarch Elizabeth Hosking Nims' 1851 wedding dress. There is one problem with this documentation; stylistically, this dress was made much later than 1851. But which Nims woman wore it? The likeliest candidate, if this is in fact a wedding or going away dress, is Alice E. Nims, who married Harding Barber in 1883.

Bowen Collection, University Museum, Accession No. 73,
Gift of the Nims Family
See also Figs. 2, 5, 46, 78, 96

Key

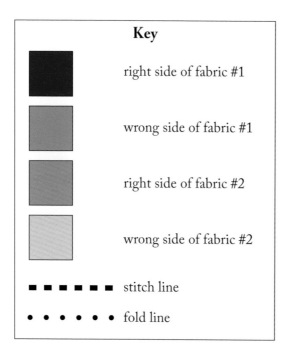

right side of fabric #1

wrong side of fabric #1

right side of fabric #2

wrong side of fabric #2

■ ■ ■ ■ ■ stitch line

• • • • • • fold line

Making Bound Edges

Materials & Supplies:
fabric
ruler
chalk
pins
scissors or rotary cutter
needle or sewing machine if project
     complexity allows
thread
steam iron

The first step in making bound edges is to make bias tape. Two different methods are shown here, a pieced method for smaller yardage needs and a continuous bias method if the project requires several yards.

Pieced Bias Method *(small yardage)*

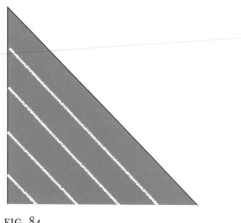

FIG. 84

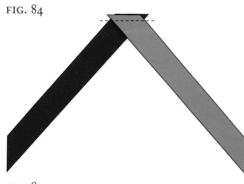

FIG. 85

1.) Choose a fabric and determine the width of the strips. Make sure to have an on-grain straight edge on top.

2.) Fold the fabric back diagonally so the straight edge lines up with the selvage. Press the fold. Mark parallel lines from the crease at the determined strip width (fig. 84). Cut the fabric.

3.) Take two strips and place them right sides together at right angles to each other. Stitch straight across leaving a ¼″ seam allowance (fig. 85).

4.) Open the seam and press, then trim away the excess fabric (fig. 86). Repeat with remaining strips.

FIG. 86

Continuous Bias Method *(large yardage)*

1.) Choose a fabric, cut a square shape, then cut the square diagonally from one corner to the other (fig. 87).

FIG. 87

2.) Place two short edges right sides together, with triangle ends overlapping equally at each end. Sew the segments together with a ¼″ seam allowance (fig. 88). Open the seam and press flat.

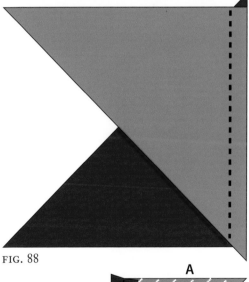

FIG. 88

3.) On the back of the fabric, use the ruler and chalk to mark cutting lines parallel to the long edges of the fabric (fig. 89).

FIG. 89

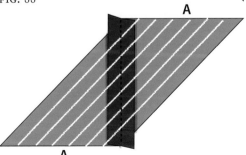

BOUND EDGES

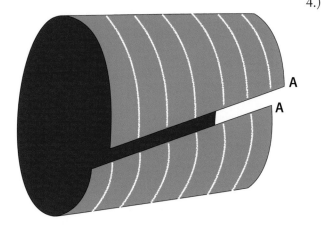

FIG. 90

4.) Form a tube by bringing the right sides of the fabric together, matching edge A to edge A. Make sure to offset the ends to make lines match up exactly, lining up the chalk marks, not the edges of the fabric (fig. 90). On either end, your chalk line should align with the cut end of the fabric. Sew the tube closed with a ¼″ seam; press open.

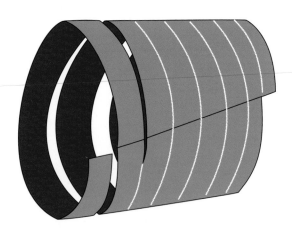

FIG. 91

5.) Cut the chalked line around the tube until there is one long strip of bias binding (fig. 91).

Bias Binding

Now that the lengths of bias are prepared, here is how to use them to make bound edges:

1.) Lay the strip on the ground fabric with right sides together. Match the raw edges and sew together (fig. 92).

FIG. 92

2.) Tightly wrap the strip over and to the back, then press (fig. 93).

3.) If the back will be exposed, turn the raw edges under, if not the edges can be left as is. Whether turned under or not, hand-sew the binding to ground fabric with catch-stitches to secure. Take care not to show stitches on the front (fig. 94).

FIG. 93

Figure 95 is a side view showing how the main fabric and the bias strip interact.

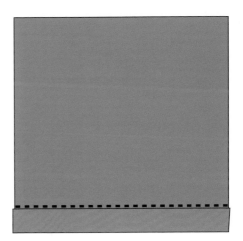

FIG. 94

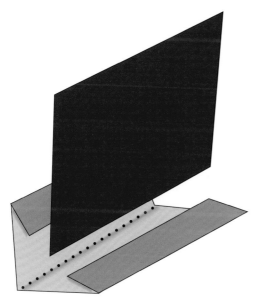

FIG. 95

Hemming Variant

Finishing a hem to the outside is a technique that resembles bound edges and is another example of the Victorian joy of embellishing everything. Usually, hems are discretely folded under and held in place with stitches almost invisible from the front. But sometimes, as illustrated in figure 96, hems become decorative instead. Turned to the outside and stitched by hand, they mimic a bound edge and add another visual feature.

FIG. 96A. *Above: View of a section of the underskirt for Plate 6 (p. 56), with a broad band decorating the hem.*

FIG. 96B. *Below: Interior view of the band, showing that it is actually simply hemmed to the front and set with hand stitches invisible from the front.*

Piping

The use of very narrow piping to finish edges, reinforce, or highlight seams is one of the most frequently found clothing details of the nineteenth century. Piping is made by folding a strip of bias-cut fabric in half around a cord and stitching up close to the cord to encase it. Because the fabric is on the bias, the piping can follow the curves and contours of a garment's seams. Some of the piping in this period is so tiny that the cord is only a thread or two thick. As the century progressed, piping disappears from seams and instead is used to draw the eye to a specific part of a gown (fig. 4), or to emphasize an edge. In some cases multiple rows of piping are used to emphasize an edge or a seam (fig. 97).

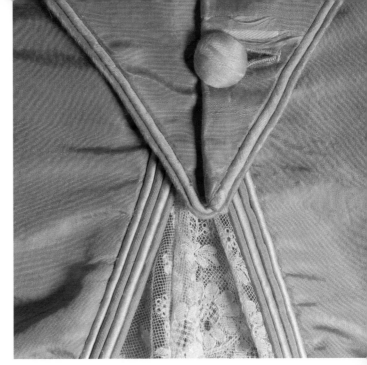

FIG. 97. *Close up detail of gown in Plate 7 (p. 64), with four stacked rows of piping on each side of the seam.*

Making Basic Piping

Materials & Supplies:
- fabric
- ruler
- chalk
- pins
- cord or gimp
- needle or sewing machine
- thread

1.) The first step is to make plenty of bias-cut strips as described on pages 58–60, figures 84–91. If not much is needed use the piece method, otherwise use the continuous method.

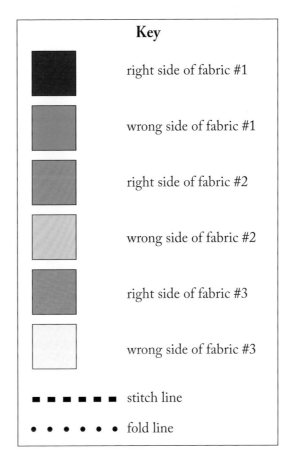

	Key
⬛	right side of fabric #1
⬛	wrong side of fabric #1
⬛	right side of fabric #2
⬛	wrong side of fabric #2
⬛	right side of fabric #3
⬜	wrong side of fabric #3
▪ ▪ ▪ ▪ ▪	stitch line
• • • • • •	fold line

Plate 7

A Colonial Revival: The Frost-Sawyer Evening Gown

1875–77
Silk taffeta and satin, lace

This silk evening gown is made of a moonlight taffeta with powder blue satin piping and lace accents. The gown is constructed of one piece although it appears to have an under-skirt, and the train is quite long. A notable embellishment gracing the overskirt is the piping, a detail usually present in a single or double row in nineteenth-century garments but here a full four rows deep at the hem, joining into an impressive eight-row-wide piping band at the center front of the overskirt just below the point of the bodice. Originally made for a trim figure, likely that of Martha Frost, a well-established lawyer's wife who would have been in her mid-thirties when the gown was fabricated, the darts shaping the bodice were let out at some later date though the sewn-in skirt waistband proved too difficult to alter as well and the dress sustained stress tears as a result.

Given the style, color, and date of the gown, it was likely influenced by the recent centennial celebrations of 1876 in Philadelphia: the pale palette echoed what was understood (given the knowledge base of the time) to be "Colonial" and the gathering of the dress at the sides of the false overskirt has echoes of the panniered gowns popular during the 1770s and 1780s and revived in the 1870s. Panniers widened skirts at the hips without adding fullness to the front or back, an effect similar to the way the fabric on this gown is treated. There was extensive, excess yardage in this type of gown which frequently indicated wealth. Unlike the structured movement seen in the Nim's dress a decade later, here the fabric itself creates an active sweep in concert with the wearer. The suggestion of the exposed underskirt indicated a pastoral idyll and leisurely lifestyle, away from court, as in a Watteau painting.

Note: A gown such as this signifies wealth and position, and the Frost (or Ffrost) Sawyer family who donated it to the University had both. Their homestead on the Oyster River is the oldest house in Durham, New Hampshire, and one of the oldest in the state; river commerce fueled family fortunes, and prosperity continued even after the railways shifted the economy.

Bowen Collection, University Museum, Accession No. 46,
Gift of Mrs. James Sawyer
See also Figs. 9, 97, 106

2.) Place a long fabric strip right side down on the work surface and lay a cord in the center. Fold the fabric over the cord, keep the cord centered, and match the raw edges of the fabric (fig. 98).

FIG. 98

3.) Sew close to the cord (fig. 99). Try using a zipper foot for this if a cording foot is not available.

FIG. 99

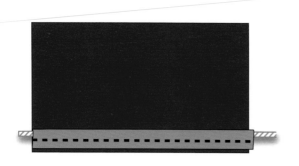

4.) Lay the piping strip on the right side of the garment, matching raw edges. To attach, sew close to the stitch line of the piping (fig. 100).

FIG. 100

If the garment is to be lined, then sandwich the piping between the fashion fabric and the lining, with the lining and fashion fabric right sides together. Sew and turn right side out (fig. 101).

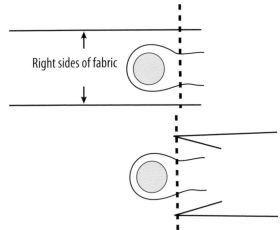

FIG. 101

5.) Fold piping over and press the seam allowance away from the piping edge and toward the garment (fig. 102).

FIG. 102

6.) If the piping is sandwiched between fashion fabric and a lining, this is a finished edge. If there is no lining, turn the raw edge of the piping under and catch-stitch it in place. This encapsulates the raw edge of the fashion fabric as well (fig. 103).

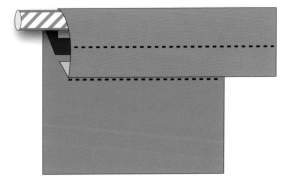

FIG. 103

BOUND EDGES

Making Multiple Piping

FIG. 104 *Exterior view*

1.) To make multiple or stacked rows of piping, position the initial piping on the fabric and then sew to the garment as in step 4 (p. 66). Place the next row of piping next to the first and sew close to the cord. It's easiest to do this by hand. Repeat for as many rows as desired (fig. 104).

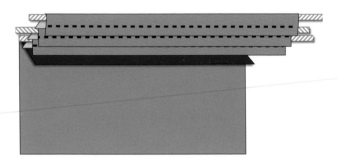

Interior view

2.) Multiple rows of piping can be finished by lining that part of the garment. Assemble the multiple piping as in Fig. 104, then sew the lining fabric by hand to the outermost piping band next to the cord, as in figure 105. After sewing in place, turn the lining so wrong sides of fabric and lining are together.

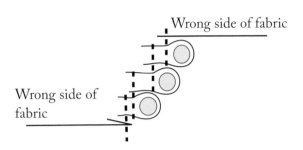

3.) Another method for finishing multiple piping is to enclose the raw edges with a plain strip of fabric (fig. 106). Sew the fabric strip to the outermost piping strip next to the cord, then flip it down toward the garment. Fold the fabric strip's raw edge under, and finish with a catch-stitch. (fig. 107).

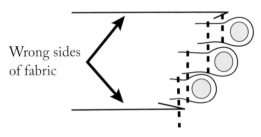

FIG. 105

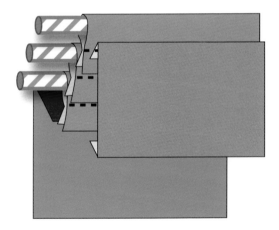

FIG. 107

FIG. 106. *Close up of the inside of the 4-wide piping strip with catch-stitches visible near the fold. See Plate 7 (p. 64).*

FIG. 108. Godey's Lady's Book, *1867*

FIG. 109. Godey's Lady's Book, *1863. Printed border mimicking soutache braid.*

6

Cord and Braid Work

This is the simplest decorative technique, but visually very dramatic, and easily applied to almost any garment or accessory. Woven cord, soutache braid, and flat braid of various widths are stitched to the ground fabric in elaborate patterns. Colors can contrast or match. This form of embellishment was so popular in the nineteenth century, and so technically accessible to all skill levels, that women's magazines routinely printed pattern samples (figs. 108 and 122). Eventually fabrics were printed to look as though cord or braid work had already been applied to them (fig. 109)!

For most of the nineteenth century this kind of handwork was painstakingly added to the finished garment either with whipstitch for cord and braid, or a running stitch for soutache braid (fig. 110). However, with the appearance of sewing machines some of this work began to be done mechanically, as is the case for the suit in Plate 8 (p. 72).

This suit has been embellished with a round woven or braided cord sewn by machine. Each piece of the coat was first cut out of the plain wool and then certain sections decorated before assembly (fig. 111). Cording, pieced together into a single continuous line, creates a meandering floral pattern, with loose ends passed through the fabric and hidden on the inside. Smaller sections of cord work applied to the velvet collar, upper sleeves, cuffs, buttons, and skirt, all by machine, complete the look.

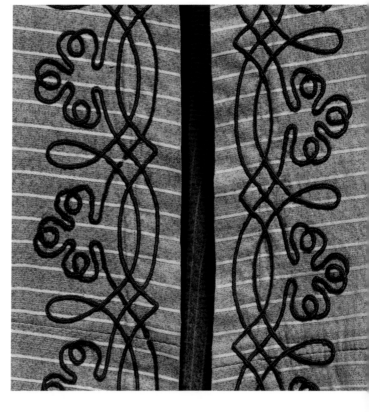

FIG. 110. *Detail of soutache border on a capelet circa 1860s, wool, Accession No. 129.*

Plate 8

Victoria Elides to Edward: Design Continuity in Kate's 1909 American Wedding Suit

1909

Worsted wool, silk velvet, and cording by Chandler & Co. Boston

While not a Victorian garment, this richly hued, deep blue suit nonetheless represents the continuation of an embellishment aesthetic into the early twentieth century. The garment itself has simple lines, but the visual luxury created by the carefully crafted tone-on-tone cord work and the lovely contrast of the velvet collar are direct descendants of a more elaborate age. Purchased at Chandler & Co., a prominent department store on Tremont Street in Boston, the suit features a combination of plain wool panels and matching machine-decorated panels, with more cord detailing on the velvet collar. Chandler sold yard goods and this suit would have been made and embellished to order. While it was a distinguished and lovely garment, it was also truly an American suit, intended for an active and stylish woman.

In comparison with the haute couture offerings illustrated by the Maison Rouff tea gown of less than a decade earlier (Plate 5, p. 44), and especially with Alice Nims' constraining two-tone gown of the 1880s (Plate 6, p. 56), it is clear how rapidly American society was changing. It would have been possible to comfortably yet stylishly walk and travel by train or streetcar wearing this garment. In fact, it was worn by Kate Lanmon Nims at her 1909 marriage to prominent lawyer and state legislator, John E. Benton. Kate was forty at the time and this fashionable suit was quite appropriate for a bride of her age. Her husband was elected mayor of Keene, New Hampshire, the following year and it is tempting to speculate that the suit was subsequently worn on numerous occasions, eventually accompanying the couple to Washington, DC upon John's election to Congress. Accessorized with boots by day and perhaps changing into heels for an evening reception, one can easily imagine Kate confidently wearing this ensemble as she assisted her husband with his political ambitions.

Bowen Collection, University Museum, Accession No. 72,
Gift of the Nims Family
See also Figs. 7, 111, 116, 118

Twisted cord, also popular, is an element of the surface treatment on the Maison Rouff Paris gown, as illustrated in Plate 5 (fig. 112). This work is an accent to an accent; the hand-sewn cords form stems from which the delicate ribbon fronds and roses spread across the skirt.

FIG. 111. *The side seam shows how the pattern is cut off by the edge of the panel. The braided cord is machine sewn.*

FIG. 112. *Hand-applied twisted cording accent for ribbon work, see Plate 5 (p. 44).*

Making Cord and Braid Work

Materials & supplies:

> soutache braid, bias-woven flat braid,
> round woven cord, twisted cord,
> or combination (fig. 113)
> pattern
> chalk or marking pencil
> embroidery hoop for small projects
> or
> needlework frame for large ones
> thread
> needle for hand sewing or sewing
> machine cording foot

Handle examples of these cords and braids before purchasing as some will be more appropriate for tight curves than others. Make sure the cord or braid characteristics fit the pattern.

> **TIP:**
> Soutache braid has two structural cords inside. Curves can be created by pulling on one or the other of these cords. This works best for small lengths of braid (fig. 113).

For hand-applied cord and soutache, the stitch used will depend on the type of cord or braid chosen: soutache, flat braid, or round woven cord requires the use a running or backstitch (fig. 114); twisted cord uses a whipstitch that wraps around the cord so that the thread nestles into the twist and disappears (fig. 115). A sewing machine requires the use of a cording foot: Victorian machine-applied cording used a straight stitch, but a zigzag stitch can be used for a different effect.

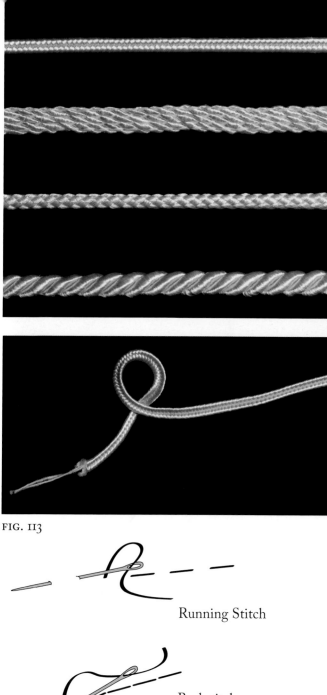

FIG. 113

Running Stitch

Backstitch

FIG. 114

Whipstitch
(wraps around
cord)

FIG. 115

FIG. 116. *Cord ends hidden in the seam.*

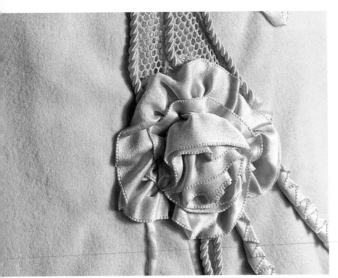

FIG. 117. *Cord ends hidden behind the rosette. See Plate 5 (p. 44).*

1.) Choose a design and transfer it to the fabric with chalk or marking pencil (Appendix for instructions).

2.) Stretch the fabric over an embroidery hoop to control the tension. Working without tensioned fabric can cause puckers in the finished piece.

3.) For beginning, ending, or piecing in more lengths of cord or braid, there are three options:

    a. Hide the ends in a seam, if the pattern allows for this (fig. 116).

    b. Design the pattern to hide ends under other parts of the embellishment. Anchor the end tightly to the fabric with a few stitches to keep it from fraying (fig. 117).

    c. Hide the ends on the inside of the garment. Use an awl to gently spread the weave of the fabric and pass the ends to the inside. There are often natural places in a design to hide an end, such as a tight corner (fig. 118).

FIG. 118. *A sharp corner in the pattern hides the end of one piece of cord and the beginning of another; both have been brought to the back of the fabric.*

4.) Anchor the cord or braid with a few stitches and start stitching it to the fabric. Go slowly and make sure to follow the pattern lines closely. Do not space the stitches too far apart, otherwise there may be gaps that can catch on things and pull the stitches loose on the final piece.

FIG. 119. *Contrasting thread used here for clarity.*

5.) When using a whipstitch on twisted cord, line the stitches up with the twists in the cord so the thread disappears into the channel (fig. 119). In general stitches can be spaced every few twists to secure the cord (fig. 120). Space stitches closer together in tight curves to control the shape.

FIG. 120

6.) When using a running or backstitch, make sure only small stitches are visible from the front, and travel with longer stitches in the back (fig. 121).

7.) Add more cord or braid as needed as described in Step 3.

8.) Finish the pattern. When hiding the cord or braid ends under parts of the design, make sure to tuck the frayed end well beneath the work and anchor it with several stitches.

> **TIP:**
> When working with twisted cord, you can give tight curves in the pattern an assist by rolling the cord lightly in your fingers first to tighten the twist, and then sew it down in that slightly torqued state.

FIG. 121. *Detail of c. 1860s wool capelet, Accession No. 129.*
Left: inside of garment, showing long stitches.
Right: outside of garment, with stitches tiny and almost invisible.

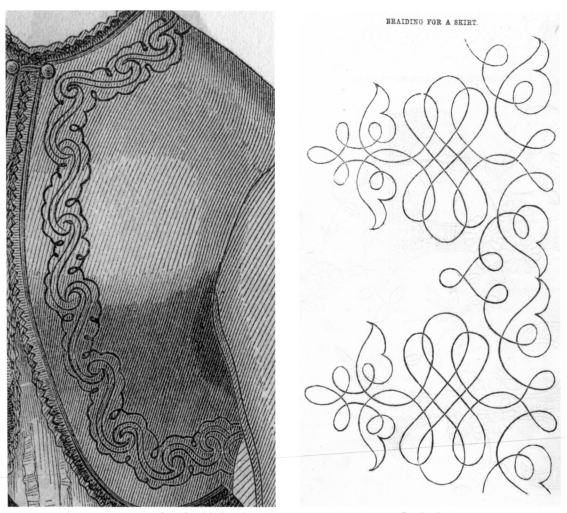

FIG. 122A *shows more examples of published braid patterns for handwork:* Godey's *1864*

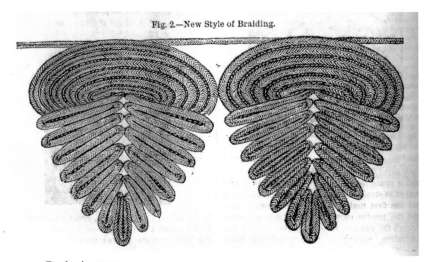

FIG. 122B. Godey's *1873*

Detail, Plate 5 (p. 44)

79

Plate 9
Art Nouveau Channeled into American Exuberance: The Sanders Coat

Circa 1894
Wool (plain weave worsted, well-fulled.)

Marcia Sanders was a single woman of about twenty when she wore this beautifully decorated, highly fashionable coat. The large sleeves are typical of exaggerated 1890s styling and the flair of the Art Nouveau style, just beginning to sweep Europe in a post-1889 Paris Exposition world. The diminutive waist—just 25 inches—is impressive considering that this heavy wool outerwear garment would have covered layers of clothing and corsetry and demanded to be buttoned snugly and smoothly. The silhouette created by a coat like this was eye-catching: the over-scaled shoulders, flowing pockets, and longer length would have crafted an illusion of height as well as emphasizing the small waist. Even the buttons are dramatically over-sized. There is something intrinsically appealing about this coat, even for contemporary designers.

The most striking feature of the coat is its intricate appliqué, gracing the cuffs, hem, front opening, collar, and center back. The fabric used to make the coat also embellishes it. Lavish and impressive as it looks, however, the technique is startlingly simple. The work completed before the garment's final assembly (with the exception of the center back element) is entirely by machine with a single thread beneath and a double thread on the surface. Each surface element is first drawn or transferred onto a piece of fabric then sewn to its intended coat section. The surface wool is then carefully trimmed away close to the stitch line, removing excess fabric and revealing the design. Because the wool is fulled, a process in which the fibers of the textile interlock with each other, edges do not fray easily even when cut. The work is painstaking, carefully lining up parts of the trailing vine over the seams for smooth transitions. The construction of the final garment is equally precise. The seams and hem are bound with strips of cotton, and even the pockets are beautifully tailored, flowing from the line of the side seams. This important wardrobe item also indicates much about the tastes and trends of young single women at the time, when the freedom to attend Cycloramas or visit the World's Columbian Exposition of 1893 placed them outside the home and frequently under male gaze.

Bowen Collection, University Museum, Accession No. 51,
Gift of Mrs. Marcia Sanders
See also Fig. 123

7

Appliqué

Appliqué is the technique of fastening a fabric shape to the surface of another piece of fabric. A number of methods can be used to achieve this effect. The impressive coat in Plate 9 (p. 80) employs the easiest method, in which topstitched shapes are cut close to the stitch line and left otherwise unfinished (fig. 123). This example is machine sewn using a double-thread stitch, such as a darning stitch on modern sewing machines. Because the fabric used is a thick fulled wool, the edges of the cut shapes do not fray.

Making Topstitched, Raw-edge Appliqué

Materials & Supplies:
- fulled wool or other non-fraying
  - fabric
- pattern
- chalk or marking pencil
- pins
- sewing machine with darning stitch
  - or
- similar thick effect setting
- thread
- sharp scissors

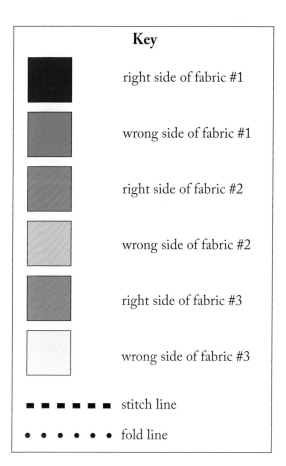

Key

- right side of fabric #1
- wrong side of fabric #1
- right side of fabric #2
- wrong side of fabric #2
- right side of fabric #3
- wrong side of fabric #3
- ▪ ▪ ▪ ▪ ▪ stitch line
- • • • • • fold line

FIG. 123. *View of the center back of the coat.*

Chain Stitch

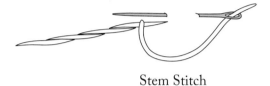

Stem Stitch

FIG. 124.

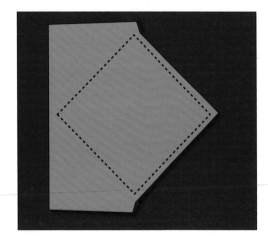

FIG. 125. *The right half of the shape has been trimmed close to the stitch line.*

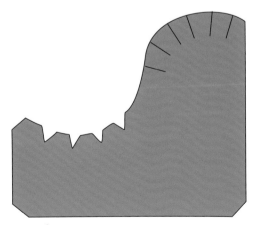

FIG. 126.

1.) Draw the pattern onto a piece of fabric. The coat in this example uses the same fabric for both garment and appliqué, but feel free to experiment with other combinations.

2.) Position the fabric onto the garment, pin firmly in place.

3.) You can choose to sew either by hand or machine. In either case, sew carefully along the pattern lines. Go slowly and be precise. If sewing by hand with a chain stitch or stem stitch, make sure to use a hoop or frame for tension control (fig. 124).

4.) Once the pattern is completely attached, take small, very sharp scissors and carefully remove the excess surface fabric close to the stitching line (fig. 125).

Making Turned-under Edge Appliqué

If you are working with a more easily frayed fabric, you will need to finish the edges of your applied pieces. You will need similar supplies as for the topstitched raw-edge method.

1.) Draw the pattern onto a piece of fabric.

2.) Cut out the applied element leaving at least a ¼″ seam allowance. Clip any round areas and corners to keep the shapes flat (fig. 126).

3.) Turn the seam allowance to the inside and press.

4.) Position the fabric onto the garment, and pin firmly in place. Sew down along the edge by machine or by hand.

Making Turned-under, Edge-finished Appliqué

Materials & Supplies:

> fabric for your applied element
> piping or cord
> pattern
> chalk or marking pencil
> pins
> sewing machine or needle
> thread

Another common Victorian appliqué technique involves finishing the raw edges of the applied element with piping (fig. 127) or bias tape. This gown uses a fabric of contrasting texture but matching color for the applied element. Feel free to experiment with other combinations.

FIG. 127. *What looks like a turned-back corner of the skirt is actually a fabric triangle of a contrasting texture applied to the surface. See Plate 2 (p. 10).*

1.) Follow the previous instructions for making piping (beginning on page 63). Sew the piping to the appliqué element, right sides together (fig. 128). Clip as with figure 126 to reduce bulk and ensure smooth curves.

FIG. 128

FIG. 129

2.) Turn raw edges to the back and press. The ends of the piping will be captured in the next step (fig. 129).

3.) To enclose the remaining raw edge as in figure 127, match raw edges of the appliqué and the garment fabric, right side of appliqué to wrong side of garment (fig. 130).

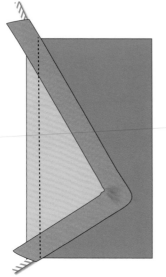

FIG. 130

4.) Press the seam open to flatten and smooth the seam. Trim excess fabric. Fold the appliqué to the right side of the fabric, pin, and "stitch in the ditch" (fig. 131) next to the cord of the piping to attach this piece to the garment as invisibly as possible (fig. 132).

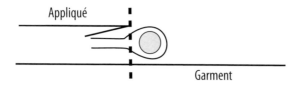

FIG. 131

FIG. 132

To add an appliqué bound by piping as illustrated in figure 140 (p. 89), the raw ends of the piping need to be enclosed. There are two common ways to do this, butted ends and overlapped ends. Butted ends are used on the example provided by figure 140 (p. 89).

Making Piping with Butted Ends

FIG. 133

1.) Sew the piping in place all around the appliqué element, right sides together, stopping within a few inches from either end. On one end, trim the cord away ¼″ from the end of the piping fabric (fig. 133).

FIG. 134

2.) Fold ¼″ of the piping fabric to the inside, creating a finished end. Lay the piping from the other end INSIDE, so that the folded edge of one side covers the raw edge of the other (fig. 134).

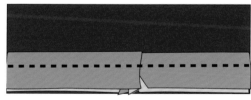

FIG. 135

3.) Stitch across the join to hold it in place (fig. 135).

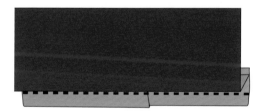

FIG. 136

4.) Turn raw edges to the inside and press (fig. 136). The appliqué can now be sewn to the garment by "stitching in the ditch" all the way around.

Making Piping with Crossed Ends

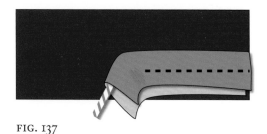

FIG. 137

1.) Sew the piping in place all around the appliqué element, right sides together, starting about ½˝ from the end of the piping on one side. Angle the loose end down toward the raw edge of the fabric (fig. 137).

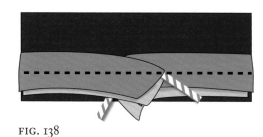

FIG. 138

2.) When you reach the other end, lay it across the first angled end, also angling it downward as shown in figure 138. Sew across both ends to secure.

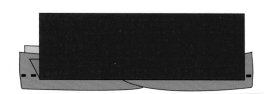

FIG. 139

3.) Turn raw edges to the inside and press (fig. 139). The appliqué can now be sewn to the garment by "stitching in the ditch" all the way around.

FIG. 140. *See Plate 2 (p. 10).*

APPLIQUE

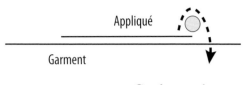

Appliqué

Garment

FIG. 141

Cord is on the
boundary, stitches
join the appliqué to
the ground fabric.

Corded Edges

As noted above, cord work can also be used to
finish an appliquéd edge. Prepare the appliqué
element as in figure 126 or it will fray. Baste
the element in place so it cannot shift while
working the cord work. Make sure the cord
or braid is right on top of the folded-under
edge and sew it down so that the element is
firmly anchored to the garment by the stitches.
At least one side of the whipstitch if not both
should pierce the appliquéd element; figure 141
shows the placement of cording and stitches.

Stitched-edge Appliqué

The last common appliqué technique for the
era is described in an 1873 project in *Godey's
Lady's Book* (fig. 142). The illustrated piece is
a letter case measuring 10″ x 5″, described as
made of a blue silk ground with a black silk
appliqué. Silk frays when cut, but this elaborate
example uses a button hole stitch of yellow silk
to bind the edges. In the illustration the finish
looks more like a blanket stitch, but it's worth
noting that *The Complete Needlepoint Guide*
(1873) refers to "buttonhole" and "blanket
stitch" as the same stitch.

FIG. 142. Godey's Lady's Book, *1873*

Making Stitched-edge Appliqué

Materials & Supplies:
    fabric for your applied element
    pattern
    chalk or marking pencil
    fusible web
    needle
    thread

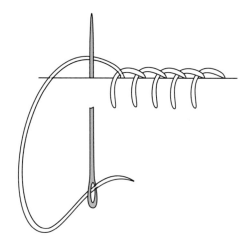

FIG. 143. *Blanket stitch*

1.) Draw or transfer the pattern onto fabric.

2.) To make working with an intricate shape easier, especially with a fabric that might fray, the use of a fusible web such as WonderUnder™ is recommended to reinforce the fabric and join it securely to the ground.

3.) Cut out your applied element.

4.) Position the appliqué onto the garment. Follow the product instructions for attaching the fusible web to the garment.

5.) Using a contrasting thread color, sew a blanket stitch (fig. 143) all around the edges of the appliqué. The fusible web will keep it in place temporarily, but the stitching ensures it will stay in place permanently as well as creating a decorative edge that won't fray (fig. 144).

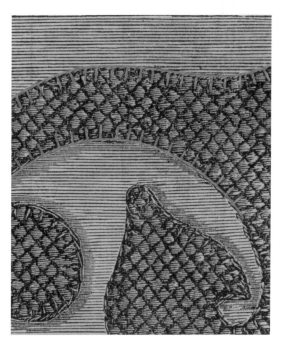

FIG. 144. *Close up of* Godey's *sample. The shape looks like a mesh because, according to the magazine's description, the silk it's cut from has a pattern to it.*

FIG. 145. *Silk fringe edging. See Plate 1 (p. 4).*

Afterword: Passementerie

We think of Victorian homes as being heavily tasseled and fringed, but the same aesthetic held for garments as well. Passementerie provides a new way to think about the home decoration department in your local fabric store. During the Victorian era all passementerie (fringe, elaborate tassels, intricate hanging cords, rosettes, and gimp) were treated as very fashionable enhancements for clothing (figs. 145–149). Some of the more outrageous dangling upholstery decorations might not be for the faint of heart, but a cascade of interesting fringe or braided cord offers an exotic and distinctive finishing touch!

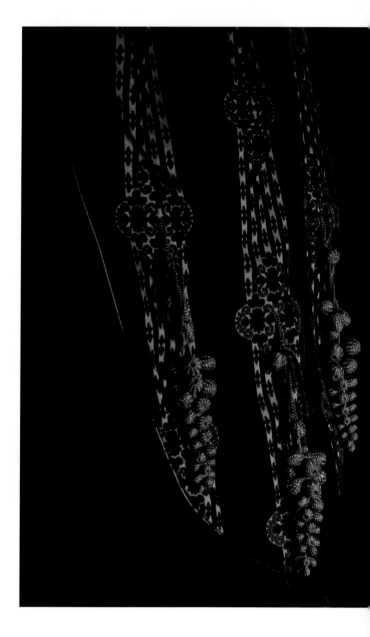

FIG. 146. *Thread-covered buttons in a grape cluster on the skirt. See Plate 10 (p. 96).*

FIG. 147. *Detail of gimp edging on the bodice and as decorative button loops. See Plate 10 (p. 96).*

FIG. 148. *Detail of chenille fringe on a dress, c.1880s, silk barège, Accession No. 108.*

AFTERWORD

Plate 10
L'Heure Bleue: A Gown of Midnight Blue Velvet

c. 1890
Silk velvet, cord, and passementerie

This sumptuous two-piece walking gown typifies Victorian construction savvy and mindset—it is all about presentation and illusion. The fabric is the true star of this gown. Every movement brings a play of texture and light in the lustrous silk velvet pile of the gown's underskirt, sleeves, and bodice. Flashes of color peek through the spectacular voided velvet panels of the overskirt and bodice front, where a rich crimson ground is woven with a deep midnight blue velvet pile in intricate patterns to look as though elaborate brocaded ribbons were cascading down the fabric. A clever play of blue and red carries through to the grape-like ball clusters on the skirt and the two-tone cording on the bodice—even the buttons have a peek-a-boo aspect, teasingly displaying a red core covered with blue thread.

Behind this glamorous façade, however, the expensive fabric of the shell barely extends past the borders of the jacket (fig. 3), and the underskirt is mostly an inexpensive cotton, with velvet sewn precisely following the contours of the overskirt. The skirt has a complex construction with an underskirt and overskirt that appear independent, but are in fact sewn together. The small train provides a perfect finale.

When placed within the context of the *Exposition Universelle*, held in Paris in 1889, which celebrated technology in the form of the soaring Eiffel Tower and luxury in the shape of the largest diamond known, the dress exemplifies optimism and success in the modern world.

Bowen Collection, University Museum, Accession No. 157
See also figs. 3, 146, 147

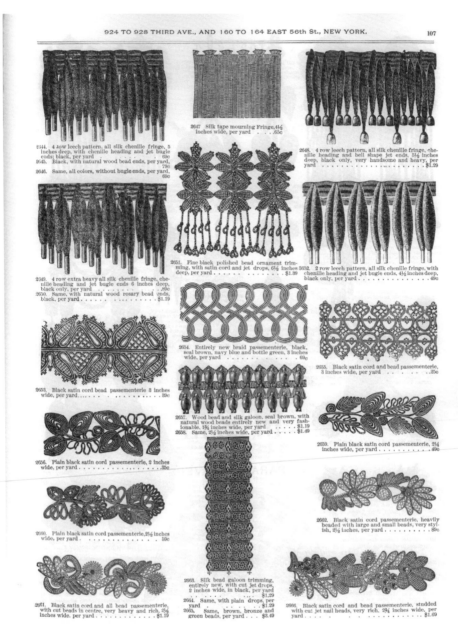

FIG. 149. *Bloomingdale's catalog, 1886, passementerie selection.*

In conclusion...

The intention behind this book is to reintroduce a richly vibrant aesthetic to contemporary design. Now that you've seen how it all goes together, you can look at Victorian clothing with a new appreciation for the design approach behind them.

And go, make beautiful things!

Glossary

Accordion pleat: one of a series of narrow, evenly spaced parallel knife pleats with alternating raised and recessed folds which allows the garment to expand its shape when moving.

Appliqué: decorative technique whereby a fabric shape is applied to the surface of the garment.

Backstitch: used both in the beginning and end of a row of stitching to anchor the thread and in areas needing strong seams; created by stepping the sewing needle back with each stitch before coming forward to reinforce the stitches, with the overlapping visible in the back of the fabric while the stitches simply touch each other from the front (see Appendix).

Baste: a long running stitch used to hold fabric in place temporarily.

Bias: a term used for fabric cut in a direction diagonal to the weave of the fabric.

Binding: encasing the raw edge of the fabric with a narrow strip of fabric, usually cut on the bias for contouring ability.

Blanket stitch: a stitch that is used to neaten and finish the cut edges of fabric (see Appendix).

Box pleat: a row of crisp folds made by alternating directions.

Braid: multiple fibers woven together into a trim by braiding them, can form a tube or be flat.

Catch stitch: a large cross-stitch used in finishing seams and hems, with each anchoring stitch catching just two or three threads of the fabric.

Chain stitch: an stitch formed by bringing the needle up from behind the fabric and down through the fabric in the same hole, leaving a loop of thread on the surface which is caught by the next stitch. Used by the first sewing machine as a construction stitch but most commonly an embroidery stitch today.

Cord: fibers formed into a structural strand either by twisting them together or by weaving or braiding them into a narrow tube.

Dagged/dags: a series of decorative scallops or foliations along the edge of a garment.

Faille: a soft, finely-ribbed fabric that can be made from cotton, silk, or man-made materials.

Inverted box pleat: a box pleat reversed so that the bulk of the material is turned to the back.

Knife pleat: a row of crisp folds running in one direction.

Passementerie: trimming used on clothing and upholstery, consisting of braids, gimps, tassels, buttons, cords, ribbons, fringes, using silks and metal threads.

Piping: an edging made by encasing thread, cord, or gimp in a bias strip of fabric.

Plain weave: a textile weave where the filling threads and the warp threads interlace, forming a checkerboard pattern.

Pleating: A fold in cloth made by doubling the material upon itself. Usually pressed to make the folds crisp and defined.

Pouf: a piece of clothing fabric gathered into a puff, creating a bulge in the center while the edges are held together.

Rolled hem: hem created by folding the raw edge under, and then folding over that amount again.

Ruching: Created by gathering fabric in a repeating pattern to form soft ruffles, scallops or pleats.

Running stitch: used for basting, by running the thread over and under the fabric; it can also be used as the basis for a more decorative stitch (see Appendix).

Satin: a textile weave that creates a lustrous front and a matte back.

Self trim: trim created with the same fabric as the garment.

Soutache: a narrow, flat herringbone braid used in trimming, made with two thick strands woven together by fine threads.

Stacked pleats: any form of pleating in which multiple pleats are made to lie on top of one another.

Stem stitch: stitch made in a similar way as the backstitch, but the overlapping is done on the front of the fabric.

Stitch in the ditch: Sewing into the top of a finished seam line from the front of the garment, making the new stitches virtually invisible. The stitch goes through all layers and holds them together.

Straight grain: the length and crosswise grain of a fabric.

Taffeta: A plain-weave silk cloth, with the same finish on the front and back.

Topstitch: A row of stitching which is visible.

Whipstitch: a stitch that passes over the edge of the fabric (see Appendix).

Appendix

Stitch Diagrams

Backstitch

Running Stitch

Whipstitch
(wraps around cord)

Stem Stitch

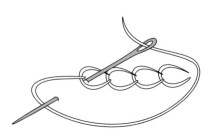

Chain Stitch

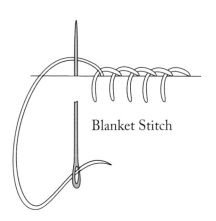

Blanket Stitch

Transferring Patterns to Fabric

There are a number of ways to mark fabric with a pattern, but it is always wise to test the method on the chosen fabric first before committing to the project. Marks should neither disappear before the project is finished, nor bleed or stain the fabric permanently. Here are three techniques:

1.) Transfer pencils such as those produced by Dritz®, Sulky® or Clover can be used to transfer the designs onto tracing paper and follow the manufacturer's instructions. When completed, iron this traced pattern onto the fabric. This type of transfer makes a mirror image of the original drawing. The marks should disappear over time but can return, so ensure the work covers the marks completely or consider a different method.

2.) Pen, graphite pencil, fabric pencil, tailor's chalk, and soapstone pencils are all choices for drawing directly on fabric. Some are removable with brushing or wetting, while others are permanent. Choose based on the needs of the design and fabric. Patterns can be drawn free-hand or traced. To trace, set the pattern beneath the fabric (easiest with light-colors) and lay this on a light box, or a glass-topped table with a lamp set beneath it, to see the pattern clearly. Trace the image.

3.) Thread can be used to baste the main lines of the pattern onto the fabric, providing a general guide.

Celestia's Inspiration?

When Celestia was deciding on the details of her dress, there were many avenues for her to get her ideas. She lived at a moment when women had more freedom and ability to create their social impressions through clothing than ever before. Sewing machines were in the process of becoming middle class trophies, recently invented commercial patterns were being produced by *Demorest's* and Butterick, among others, and fashion magazines like *Godey's*, and *Harper's Bazar* not only featured fashion plates and detailed descriptions, but sold full-sized patterns of the dresses shown in each issue. *Godey's* even provided the extra service of buying dressmaking supplies for customers.

   While there really is no way to know precisely where Celestia got the ideas for her dress, this fashion plate from the March 21, 1874, issue of *Harper's* bears striking similarities to what she made. That the dresses are not identical could mean this was not her source, or could mean she simply made other finishing choices. As this book has shown, she would have had many.

Garments and Period Print Resources

No. 31, c. early 1880s, wool twill and silk satin ribbon. Gift of Daisy Deane Williamson

No. 46, 1875-77, silk taffeta with satin and lace. Gift of Mrs. James Sawyer

No. 51, 1894, wool. Gift of Mrs. Marcia Sanders

No. 57, c. 1880, silk satin and taffeta

No. 72, 1909, wool, velvet, silk, and cording, by Chandler & Co. Boston. Gift of the Nims Family

No. 73, c. 1883, silk taffeta. Gift of the Nims Family

No. 114, early 1870s, silk faille. Gift of B. Freeman

No. 157, 1890, velvet, cord, and passementerie

No. 177, c. 1990, wool, silk, lace, net. Made by Maison Rouff

No. 2000.1, c. 1890, silk faille. Gift of Dorothy and Walter J. Peterson Jr.

Partial Views

No. 29, c. 1870s, day dress, silk taffeta

No. 71, c. 1850, jacket, watered silk

No. 76.2, day dress, silk

No. 108, 1880s, overdress, silk barège and chenille fringe

No. 129, 1860s, cape, wool and soutache

No. 227, 1870s, mourning dress, watered silk and velvet. Gift of Mrs. James Sawyer

No. 681, c. 1850, day dress, silk

Period Print Resources

Bloomingdale's catalog, 1886

Godey's Lady's Book, 1863, 1864, 1867, 1869, 1873

Harper's Bazar, 1874

Hecklinger's Ladies' Garments, 1886

Photography Credits

Photography courtesy of Lisa Nugent:
Fig. 7, 9, 15, 19, 37, 42, 43b, 50b, 56-57, 61, 77-78, 106, 118, 121, pp. 108–109, 111

Photography courtesy of Brian Smestad:
Plates 1–10

Figs. 1-6, 10–14, 16, 31-32, 38-39, 43a, 48-50a, 51, 62, 64-66, 73, 79, 80-83, 97, 110–113, 117, 123, 127, 140, 145–148, pp. 15, 79

Instructional graphics by Astrida Schaeffer

Exhibition Views

University Museum, University of New Hampshire
September 2012 – March 2013
Astrida Schaeffer, exhibition curator

EXHIBITION VIEWS

About the Author

Astrida Schaeffer has been working with historic fashions and textiles for over twenty-five years as a curator, mannequin maker, reproduction dressmaker, researcher, teacher and author. Her hands-on experience with historical reproductions has given her a detailed understanding of how clothing in museum collections works, and therefore of what each garment needs in a mannequin in order to look its best for its period. Her mannequins have appeared in museums across New England and beyond and have been published in several books. She holds two Master's degrees and was assistant director at the University of New Hampshire Museum of Art for ten years, where she was responsible for collections care, exhibition installation, and object preparation. She trained in mannequin production at the Textile Conservation Center in Lowell, Massachusetts, and with the Northern States Conservation Center, and has rehoused and inventoried costume collections for the Brick Store Museum in Kennebunk, Maine, and the University Museum at UNH. She most recently curated and prepared the mannequins for the exhibition *Embellishments: Constructing Victorian Detail*, the inspiration for this book.